THE ARCADIA STORY

Marjorie H. Russell

with
Will Hawes, Linda Hawes,
and
Elizabeth Edwards

TO SOW THE FALLOW SOIL

Winston-Derek Publishers, Inc.
Pennywell Drive—Post Office Box 90883
Nashville, Tennessee 37209

First printing

Scripture passages are from the King James version of the Bible.

1-89

BR1700.2.R83   1985   209'.2'2   [B]   85-40651
ISBN 0-938232-83-5

PUBLISHED BY WINSTON-DEREK PUBLISHERS
Nashville, Tennessee 37205

Printed in the United States of America

As God-covenanted people we dedicate this book to our Lord and Savior, Jesus Christ, whose living presence speaks to the hearts of all mankind.

The Founding Threesome—1973

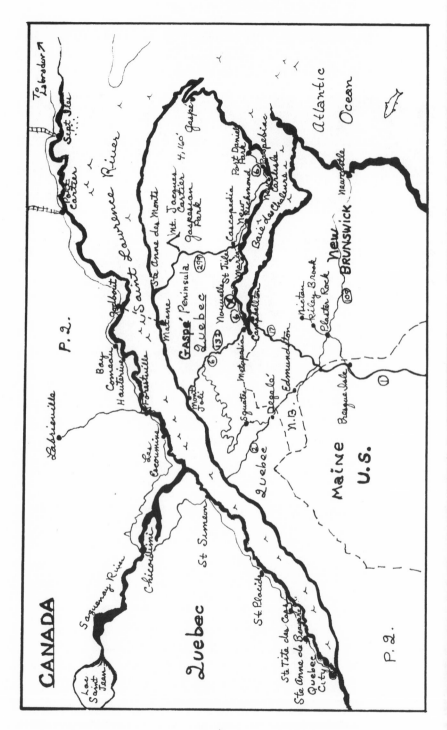

CONTENTS

PREREQUISITES

These are the prophetic checkpoints used in locating the property the Lord had designated. Each one was perfectly fulfilled.

1. Go northward and east.
2. To Canada!
3. In a valley, long, flat, and fertile.
4. Rimmed on three sides by mountains.
5. Our own mountain is E (east) of house.
6. Mixed foliage on mountain—evergreens and deciduous.
7. House is brick, two stories with two-story brick extension.
8. Tallish man and robust, short woman living in house and owning it.
9. The man and woman would walk out of the back extension door to greet Marjorie on arrival.
10. The price to the penny.
11. Would locate it in fall and arrange to buy.
12. Move into it in the spring.
13. This will be agreeable with present owners.
14. Sheep previously raised there.
15. Vegetables previously raised include asparagus ("asperge"), turnips, potatoes, carrots, beets, beans, onions.
16. Grains previously raised include wheat, barley, oats, rye, and buckwheat.
17. Soy would be new.
18. Beyond the water banks.
19. The "special" front door.
20. Mountain waterfalls, streams, fountains (springs).
21. Had to be in location as shown on map given by Lord.
22. House on rise—vantage point from which Marjorie would know this was the brick house.
23. Cedar trees abounding on property.

These were given during and after the first search:

24. Will's tractor.
25. River boundary line.
26. River unnoticed from road.
27. Brick post office on main highway.
28. Valley road leading off main highway.

INTRODUCTION

The Arcadia Story is a message of united oneness; therefore it would have been impossible for me to write it without input from "the family." Will and Linda had an important part to present, as did Betsy, now a bilingual college sophomore; Benjamin, a deep-voiced young man entering French high school; John Andrew, seven, and Samuel David, six—and there was the invaluable help of Elizabeth, our precious added family member.

We experienced great delight as we recalled the events that unfolded through our covenant with the Lord, Jesus Christ. The past twelve years have been busy ones, as we labored to found a worldwide healing prayer ministry and prepared ourselves as individuals to lead this work. We have made human mistakes, been unwise and misunderstood at times, and occasionally missed our priorities while busying ourselves with things of a secondary nature. But we have remained anchored in the Lord's initial command, and what we have given, we have given sincerely, in love. Fortunately, God judges by the intent of the heart!

Some names in the story have been changed or initials have been used; however, the facts stand true to our combined records and memories. I have mentioned only a few of the many dear ones who have touched Arcadia as well as those we have known only by mail or have met on field trips. All have shared an important place in Arcadia's prayers and work, and in our hearts. It is beautiful to see the Holy Spirit at work in them, and we rejoice and praise God when good reports of their spiritual progress reach us.

Although we still retain our strong ties with the United States, this book would not be complete without a word of gratitude to the beautiful country of Canada and the citizens of our town of Nouvelle, who so kindly welcomed us and have helped us through the years.

In retrospect, the laughter and rejoicing far outweighed the problems and difficult assignments which, at times, appeared mountainous. Our feet have often stumbled, but we remain grateful for it all, for through these experiences we have been forced to "come up higher" and closer to that infinite love that will never let us go.

Marjorie H. Russell

CHAPTER ONE

God Is Real!

NOW THE LORD HAD SAID UNTO ABRAM, GET THEE OUT OF THY COUNTRY, AND FROM THY KINDRED, AND FROM THY FATHER'S HOUSE, UNTO A LAND THAT I WILL SHEW THEE. . . . AND I WILL BLESS THEM THAT BLESS THEE, AND CURSE HIM THAT CURSETH THEE: AND IN THEE SHALL ALL FAMILIES OF THE EARTH BE BLESSED. SO ABRAM DEPARTED, AS THE LORD HAD SPOKEN UNTO HIM (Genesis 12:1,3-4a).

BUT I HAVE SAID UNTO YOU . . . I WILL GIVE IT UNTO YOU TO POSSESS IT, A LAND THAT FLOWETH WITH MILK AND HONEY; I AM THE LORD YOUR GOD, WHICH HAVE SEPARATED YOU FROM OTHER PEOPLE (Leviticus 20:24).

FEAR THOU NOT; FOR I AM WITH THEE: BE NOT DIS-MAYED; FOR I AM THY GOD: I WILL STRENGTHEN THEE . . . WITH THE RIGHT HAND OF MY RIGHTEOUS-NESS (Isaiah 41:10).

These words from the Bible stayed with Marjorie, Linda, Will, and the children throughout their long search during much of September 1972. Surely, many times they might have feared, but the courage of the Lord was fresh daily as they meditated upon Him. Such was the case on this particular night.

It was late and the stars must have been shining, but they couldn't be seen because of the dense clouds of black flies. In the absence of motels, Will had turned off the highway, making a sharp right turn onto an old wood road that plunged steeply down an incline and over a rickety bridge. Alder bushes and briars scraped the new Dodge station wagon as he accelerated to climb the hill ahead. The overhanging tree branches showed the remains of a trail unused for many years. Marjorie and Linda held on to the children—Betsy, six, and Benjamin, two—and prayed the car would be able to get out in one piece in the morning.

At the top of the rise the car lights revealed a small clearing. Wonderful! They would pitch their tent and camp there for the night. The family breathed a deep sigh of relief. As the car doors opened, the two children and the dog eagerly sprang out and the black flies sprang in. This must have been those flies' first feast in years! They made the most of it. In a matter of minutes Will was covered with welts, but Marjorie remained calm and peaceful.

"How come you aren't being bitten?" Will queried.

"You have to love them," she replied. "Remember, one of our Lord's important commandments is to love our enemies!"

"These are my enemies all right," Will muttered. His hands flew as he tried to slap his neck, head, legs, and arms all at the same time. "Mean ones, at that!"

"If you love them, they won't hurt you," Marjorie patiently explained as they unloaded the camp stove and set it up.

The children found flashlights and fetched the grocery box and helped Linda fry bacon and eggs while Will and Marjorie set up the large tent that would hold the five of them, plus the dog, Sparkie. Never since have bacon and eggs tasted as good as on that weary night in the midst of spruce- and balsam-scented air.

At last the stove was put out, the dishes packed away, and Marjorie, Will, Linda, and the children bedded down for a deep night's sleep. This was their first camping experience on the long search.

The long search for what? you might ask. The search for the special property the Lord, Jesus Christ, had told them by word and vision to seek, buy, and use for His special purposes. He had let them know in no uncertain terms that the property was in Canada—but Canada is a very large country in which to find one particular house and a certain valley edged by mountains, with all

2

the other prerequisites given by the Lord in His call, "Come out from amongst them and follow Me!" The Lord's specifications had been precise. The place had to be exactly right in every detail. There could be no facsimile.

This adventure had started almost a year earlier, after a very simple request made by Linda (Will's wife, Marjorie's daughter).

"Mom," she had asked casually one day, "I want to learn how to meditate on the Lord's Holy Word. Will you practice with me and show me how?"

"Of course," Marjorie had replied. Marjorie loved the Bible and delighted in meditating on the Lord and His Word. She was a devout pray-er and minister, having taught classes in Christian meditation and other biblical subjects for many years. The Lord had given her extensive preparation for what lay ahead.

Marjorie, raised by Christian parents in rural Massachusetts, loved nature and the out of doors and had always hungered to be closer to God. In her early twenties she met and married a wonderful young man, Garland Russell, a school principal in a nearby town.

In 1942, Marjorie's first child, Linda was delivered by major surgery. Five years later, against the doctor's advice, she had a second child, Virginia, and almost died from complications and loss of blood. In her weakened state Marjorie contracted pneumonia in the hospital and because of overcrowded conditions was sent home to recover. But the pneumonia spread to the other lung, and it seemed she would never get well.

Marjorie finally gave up the local doctor's medication and depended upon prayer alone. As the months passed, she became more and more despondent and gave up all hope of a continued worldly existence. She felt assured, however, of a future with God, and she clung to Him tenaciously.

At this point her husband, Garland, was appointed to a higher position and they moved to another city. During Marjorie's prolonged illness, a nurse and a housekeeper had been hired, but after the move, because of the tremendous financial burden, they did not hire help, except for someone who came in the mornings, and Garland did most of the work himself.

3

Marjorie was weak, but not entirely helpless. By leaning on the furniture she could move from room to room if necessary. When Garland came home at noon, he would care for the baby and fix Marjorie's lunch, and she would stay in bed until he returned at night. After school Linda usually visited playmates until supper time.

One afternoon in the early spring of 1948, Marjorie asked Garland to leave her in an easy chair instead of helping her to bed. Alone, she read her Bible, searching for help, then laid it down and gave up. Memories of the Lord's rich blessings during the previous years in His beautiful world swept over her. She thanked Him from a deeply grateful heart. She was so humbled by His goodness, she really didn't mind dying!

Sighing in desperation, she closed her eyes and prayed: "Thank You, dear Father, for all the goodness You have poured into my life—but now, dear Father, please take me home. I am no use to my dear husband or family. I am no use to anyone, including myself. I'm just a problem for everyone. Please take me home, Father. I give myself totally to You." She meant every word. Then she waited, fully expecting the loving Father to take her.

Marjorie relates, "It is only through the grace of God that this testimony is possible, because I, myself, had done nothing to merit the experience that followed. Suddenly I was carried high into the very presence of God. SUDDENLY THERE SHONE FROM HEAVEN A GREAT LIGHT ROUND ABOUT ME (Acts 22:6). That is the light I was drawn into. His light penetrated my soul. I felt his great love, also, almost like a magnet, drawing me higher and higher to His glorious throne. There was no doubt about it—I stood before His judgment seat. It was as though a two-edged sword had been thrust into my inner being and slowly turned, exposing every lack and sin. In fearsome awe and deep repentance, I realized the many times I had neglected to give love when I could have, and I asked forgiveness. To my great relief I felt God's forgiving grace baptizing me—and I was born again before the throne.

"As God healed my inner being, I could sense the atoms of my outer physical body going into place—click, click, click. From head to toe, they were moving into proper alignment. Then I was

4

moved higher into the realm of the Absolute. The glory and the majesty of God were beyond all imagining as His love engulfed me. I knew God as love and light! The Bible confirms this: GOD IS LIGHT, and IN HIM IS NO DARKNESS AT ALL (I John 1:5*b*). God had called me out of darkness into His marvelous light! The peace that passes understanding—joy beyond ecstasy, wisdom surmounting earthly intellect—became mine.

"For hours the Father taught me about Himself and about my own identity. The truth about the relationship between the Creator and His creation became apparent. I knew that God was all in all and that He is present, not only where people go after death, but here and now.

I AM GOD, AND THERE IS NONE ELSE (Isaiah 46:9).

I AM ALPHA AND OMEGA, THE FIRST AND THE LAST (Revelation 1:11).

AM I A GOD AT HAND, SAITH THE LORD, AND NOT A GOD AFAR OFF? CAN ANY HIDE HIMSELF IN SECRET PLACES THAT I SHALL NOT SEE HIM? SAITH THE LORD. DO NOT I FILL HEAVEN AND EARTH? SAITH THE LORD (Jeremiah 23:23,24).

"God taught me many heavenly truths that cannot be revealed. Then I received His anointing as the Holy Spirit set me on fire with the zeal and Spirit of the Lord. I was ordained and instructed by God to return to earth to teach and heal humankind. Alas! I did not want to leave the blissful, heavenly realm of perfection and joy. Must I return to earth? The answer came firmly, permitting no argument. He was commissioning me to return to serve Him and I knew I must go.

"In the distance, I heard a faint tinkling. The sound was repeated, growing louder each time. Gradually I consciously realized that it was the telephone. Should I answer it, or remain with God forever?

"Humanly, it was a tremendous decision. Yet I must obey God! I arose and answered the phone, and at the end of the conversation

I was aware that I had walked directly and swiftly to the other end of the room, something I had not been able to do for a long time! As I stood there amazed, I realized I had received a healing. In fact, I felt wonderful—better than I had ever felt in my life!

"Oh, God was so GOOD! My heart sang as I went to get the baby from her crib. But my vision was blurred. What was wrong with my eyes? I removed the glasses I had always worn and discovered that I could see fine without them. Praise God, my eyes had also been healed! This was later confirmed by an oculist who said I had perfect vision.

"I got the baby up, bathed and dressed her, then bathed and dressed myself and prepared dinner for my family. Phrases from the Psalms sang in my heart: BLESS THE LORD, O MY SOUL, AND FORGET NOT ALL HIS BENEFITS: WHO FORGIVETH ALL THINE INIQUITIES; WHO HEALETH ALL THY DISEASES; WHO REDEEMETH THY LIFE FROM DESTRUCTION: WHO CROWNETH THEE WITH LOVINGKINDNESS AND TENDER MERCIES (Ps. 103:2-4).

"When my husband came home from work, I ran to the door, threw it wide, and gave him a vibrant greeting and hug. Almost fainting from shock, he staggered to the couch and sat down. Surveying me standing there so ecstatic was more than he could comprehend. But as I shared my experience with him, he agreed that God certainly must have done this miraculous work. Jesus said, 'A GOOD TREE CANNOT BRING FORTH EVIL FRUIT, NEITHER CAN A CORRUPT TREE BRING FORTH GOOD FRUIT' (Matthew 7:18). My husband judged the tree by its fruit and found it very good! Together we rejoiced! When Linda came home, how wonderful for her to find a healthy, happy mother!"

From the time of her illumination, Marjorie has been aware of God's continued teaching, guidance, and power in her daily life. Gradually neighbors and friends heard of her miraculous recovery and came for prayer and healing help. It was a time of great gladness. O TASTE AND SEE THAT THE LORD IS GOOD: BLESSED IS THE MAN [or woman] THAT TRUSTETH IN HIM (Ps. 34:8).

This happened at a time when the possibility of divine healing was coming into the consciousness of more and more people, but there were few who understood what had happened to Marjorie. She found the biblical words true—that God: MAKETH . . . HIS MINISTERS A FLAMING FIRE (Ps. 104:4). She felt constantly on fire with the zeal of the Lord and found it very difficult to wait for the time when she could go forth and minister in the name of the Lord on a full-time basis.

Although the Lord had given her understanding in philosophy and theology, she realized it would be necessary to train in the practical aspects of ministering. She found it difficult to locate a theological seminary where she might learn these techniques without being bound by worldly ritual and human doctrines, even as in the days of Jesus. As her search progressed, it became obvious that the title "Christian," of itself, did not mean a thing. To be a true Christian, it is necessary to *live* love, not just talk about it.

After seven years of searching and praying, Marjorie found the right combination of studies—a combination that would allow her to be away from her family as little as possible and give her the help she sought, but still leave her free to express the truth God had taught her. Her beloved husband and parents helped her receive training from a nondenominational school, which lovingly allowed her freedom of expression. They respected the gifts God had bestowed upon her and diligently strove to cooperate with her.

On the eve of her graduation from ministerial school, the Lord, Jesus Christ, suddenly appeared to her. Looking tenderly into her soul, His all-knowing love reached into the very depths of her being. It was a divine love that would never let her go. In those brief moments of tender communication, He gave her to understand that her illuminating experience within the Godhead had been made possible by the sacrifice of His blood and body on earth. Without that sacrifice, she could never have had that experience. He let her know also that He was responsible for everyone who has ever had such an experience, whether they realize it or acknowledge it. His sacrifice in their behalf will be recognized by one and all before the end of the world.

By 1958, two years before her husband's passing, Marjorie had launched into a full-time ministry for God and was ordained by

Unity School of Christianity in 1961. Many useful years of service followed: four years of city ministry; four years at Unity Headquarters in the prayer department, teaching, writing, and counseling, as well as praying; five years as an independent minister. She taught lay leaders in Great Britain, traveled and lectured throughout America and Europe, and wrote for various publications. Finally she returned to preach and teach in Massachusetts and moved next door to Will and Linda. Will's background was quite different from Linda's. Their stories follow.

CHAPTER TWO

Will's Story

Sudbury, Massachusetts, had been my home since my birth in April 1939. I was the third child in a family of four and lived on what had developed into a twenty-five-acre estate, including two sets of greenhouses, three dwellings, and a man-made pond. We also had several fields and patches of woods.

"The place," as we called the property, was the result of a great deal of hard work by my parents and a few others. My mother, a short woman of Finnish descent, was even-tempered, kind, and a very hard worker. In the greenhouse, she specialized in bunching the flowers for sale. Her wizardry with the flowers facilitated my dad's work as a salesman in the Boston Flower Exchange. He often was up at 3:30 A.M. preparing the load for market. After returning home around noon, he spent the afternoon working in the greenhouses. In the evenings he watched the boilers to make sure the greenhouses stayed warm enough.

My grandmother on my mother's side, Aiti (Aiti means *mother* in Finnish), lived at our house and did the cooking, cleaning, and washing and cared for the children while my mother worked in the greenhouse. Aiti was also a short woman who, like my mother, worked hard but never complained and always had a cheerful disposition. Her kindness and love were like a wellspring that never ran dry.

Domenic was the greenhouse foreman. He was of Italian extraction and could outwork any three men I ever knew. In 1939 a particularly violent hurricane struck the East Coast and blew down all the greenhouses. Dad told Domenic he would have to let him go because there was no insurance to cover the losses, and there didn't seem to be any way to keep going. Dom said he would stay on and help Dad rebuild, even if he weren't paid.

For a child, "the place" offered many diversions. I could walk in the fields, roam the woods, swim in the pond, or engage in some sort of "work." I was always encouraged to work, but never forced. My folks were busy, but Dad always took time to answer my endless questions, and Mom would bake goodies or take me places. I didn't feel any pressing need to get out and socialize, so I appreciated the solitude and quiet I found at home.

When I was quite young, Dad bought an Allis Chalmers tractor. It was a small one, but I thought it was the most beautiful thing I had ever seen. Whenever Dad took it out I *had* to ride on it with him. When I was four, Dad let me take my first solo drive. As we were going slowly down the road, pulling the disc harrows, he asked me if I would like to 'drive.' Naturally I said YES, so he put the tractor in low gear, with the throttle almost closed. Then he jumped off and went farther down the road to talk to Domenic. When I arrived he climbed back on and took over, but now *I* was a driver.

At that tender age and small size, my confidence somewhat exceeded my skill. The result was that not too long afterward, an incident occurred that caused a lot of concern among the grownups. My mother had taken Aiti and me for a ride in the car and had stopped at a neighbor's house for a moment. She parked the car on a hill, leaving it in gear, but did not set the emergency brake. With Aiti in the back seat, I decided to practice my shifting. Sure enough, neutral was where I thought it should be, but suddenly the car started to roll backward down the hill toward the pond which lay far at the bottom. Naturally, Aiti became excited, as she knew nothing about cars, but I, not being able to reach the brake pedal, turned the wheel so that the car went off the road onto a level lawn. Soon it came to a stop, as I knew it would, and I couldn't figure out why all the people raced to our rescue when I, a four-year-old driver, had everything under control.

When I was five, Dom needed someone to drive the truck in the field while the men picked up rocks. He elected me. I was not at all fond of the old Model A, since I had seen it catch on fire a couple of times, but Dom never left one much choice. I was too short to see out through the windshield or to reach the floor pedals, but the old truck cab didn't have a roof or doors so I leaned out the side to see where I was going. The hand throttle provided the means to regulate the speed, and I soon learned to turn the key to turn off the motor if I got into trouble.

Eventually I drove the other trucks—the Ford and the Chevy—but the tractor remained my favorite. I loved tractors! My driving was limited, at the ages of six, seven, and eight, because no matter how hard I tried I couldn't stretch my legs enough to reach the clutch and brake.

My size and driving habits sometimes also created problems for the neighbors. One day I was driving the Model A past a neighbor's house, looking out the side as usual, when I saw her suddenly tear out of the house, a look of terror on her face, snatch up her two-year-old son from the yard, and run back inside. Later I learned she had seen the truck, but hadn't seen me, and had thought the truck was running wild.

My schooling began at the famous "Mary Lamb" School which Henry Ford had moved into Sudbury. There were sixteen pupils, in grades one through four. School didn't seem much of a challenge, and I skipped grade three because grade four work was more interesting. I was always able to get by with so little studying that by the time I reached high school, my parents were beginning to think I needed a more disciplined school environment, so I left Sudbury High and entered Tabor Academy for two years of college preparatory work. That was my first real experience of being away from home, and the instructors there saw to it that I worked hard. My grades were good, and when I finished I was accepted at both colleges to which I applied.

Thinking I would eventually take over the greenhouse business, Dom suggested that engineering would prove very useful. That sounded reasonable to me, so in 1957 I entered the University of Massachusetts to study mechanical engineering.

At the convocation on opening day, the dean of the School of Engineering said, "Only one in three of you will graduate as an engineer." I thought, "Well, if that is true, then I will be the one."

But although I was an able student, I was undisciplined in study. At Tabor I had had no choice, at the university I had many choices, and six or seven hours a day with the books wasn't one of them. After seven semesters, the university suggested I try something else.

My time spent in college was not all lost, however. Much of the engineering training I received has stayed with me, and during my last year, I met Linda, who later became my wife. My next-door neighbor, Pat, was Linda's roommate, and one day I mentioned I was looking for a date. Pat suggested Linda, but warned me she was a minister's daughter and I had better be a good boy. I did not really have any set ideas about religion in general, but I thought perhaps I *had* better be careful—if there was a God, He would certainly be looking out for a minister's daughter.

My religious life had never been very strong. My parents wanted me to go to Sunday school, so I attended a nearby church because it gave perfect attendance pins—and besides, it was closer to home than the family Methodist church. I also attended an occasional marriage and funeral service, but I couldn't really become interested in what I considered a social club. If God really existed, He wasn't real to me.

Linda and I found each other's company very enjoyable, as if we had known each other a long time. She was always very kind and did not try to press any form of religious belief on me. I was dating other girls, and for a long time I had no serious intentions toward Linda, but at the end of the school year a strange thing happened. I had enlisted in the Navy because my draft into the army would have been imminent since I was no longer in college. I knew I would be in the Navy for four years, so I bought a fraternity pin and asked Linda if she would wear it. I guess I was a bit clumsy, because afterward she said, "Whew! I thought you were going to ask me to marry you!" It was at this point that I even began to consider the idea of marriage.

In October 1961 I entered the Navy and went from the Great Lakes to Tennessee for electronics school. It was then I decided that Linda should be my wife, and I bought an engagement and a wedding ring. Finally I was stationed in San Diego, California, in a utility squadron that provided target services for the Pacific Fleet. Things were busy in the early 1960s—there was the Cuban missile crisis, President Kennedy was assassinated, and Vietnam was heating up.

When Linda and I became engaged, we decided that she should finish college, no matter what. We were married in 1962, and she graduated in 1964 with a Bachelor of Arts in Education. She taught school our last year in California before we returned East.

One thing my Navy life had taught me—I needed a college degree no matter what the cost! In 1965 I returned to the University of Massachusetts and in 1967 received a degree in management. My second round in college was much different from the first. This time I had to pay the bills, not my folks, I worked instead of playing sports, and I also had to maintain very good grades in order to graduate. Add to this the fact that now I had a wife, and in 1966 our daughter Betsy was born, and you can see that things were very different indeed.

During my last year in college I took a series of government Management Intern exams. I scored very well and received a number of telegrams and letters with very good job offers. After lengthy consideration, I decided once and for all to remain at the greenhouses, and for the next five years my life consisted of work, sports, and dabbling in local politics. My course of life was fixed, or so I thought.

It was into this setting that my mother-in-law, Marjorie, suddenly arrived. I liked her well enough, but one always has to be careful around a minister. Linda was glad to be closer to her mother and often helped with her church activities. Fortunately 'the place' needed to be tended on Sunday—flowers never take a day off—so I had an excuse to be absent from her services. To keep peace in the family, I did attend one series of Marjorie's meditation classes, without too much positive result. But even though I didn't know God, He knew me.

Linda, however, knew God quite well. Her story follows.

CHAPTER THREE

Linda's Story

My mother's contact with God had a profound effect upon my life. I observed her sudden change, but at the age of five, I was too young to understand what had happened. I was in a world of my own, wondering what I would be when I grew up. Would I be a teacher, a musician, a helper of people? My father had become a university professor, one of my grandfathers had been a Baptist missionary in the Philippines, and the other was a commercial artist. But what would I be?

About that time, Mom heard me composing a little two-phrase piece on the piano, so she and Dad decided I should take piano lessons. My teacher propped me up on two big pillows so I could reach the keyboard—but forgot the pedals.

Mom and Dad always encouraged my musical ability, and I continued into my mid-teens, taking lessons and composing. From the time I was nine, I entered talent shows, played the piano on radio, and even had my own local television show. With each public performance I had the jitters. I thought, "What if I make a mistake?" But when there were mistakes, I just kept going. The audience enjoyed hearing and seeing young people perform. I had guests who played the violin, the flute, or another instrument, solo or with my piano accompaniment. The other children were as nervous as I, and the studio temperature bothered us all; I felt like a boiled lobster under the hot lights. But my parents explained that each public performance would benefit me in years to come, and this has proved to be true.

At the Conservatory of Music in Bangor, Maine, I was taught piano theory and composition and later went on to study the pipe organ. A local church asked me, when I was fifteen, to be their organist and I accepted. That was the beginning of my professional service, and since then I have played in many churches of various denominations.

I had a happy childhood, with a younger sister and many friends to keep me company wherever we lived. But while Will was living in one house in one town and growing up with the same classmates year after year, I was on the move. As Dad climbed the professional ladder, we moved many times and I entered many new schools.

We stayed in Maine for several years, and during the fifth and sixth grades I spent many enjoyable nights at pajama parties with my classmates. We took turns visiting one another's houses. One night a friend ran short of beds. Because I was so small, she pulled two overstuffed chairs together and I slept in them comfortably, with room to spare. My seventh- and eighth-grade summers were filled with fun on our farm, jumping in the hay with city friends who found country life quite a novelty, picking wild strawberries, swimming in frigid coastal waters, and romping in the fields. My sister and I loved to climb the old gnarled apple trees. We would pick the green apples and salt them well before eating them.

During my freshman year in high school, my father was eligible for a year's sabbatical and our whole family took to car and suitcases, journeying to several parts of the country. Travel was broadening as well as exciting and educational but that year my algebra grade suffered from four school transitions.

Math was not my forte, in spite of the fact that it was Dad's. Language was more to the liking of my artistic nature—four years of Latin and French. Latin has been long forgotten, but later on, French was to come in very handy.

My question of what I would do when I grew up answered itself. As a child, I always played "teacher." There was a large blackboard in my room, and I would drill my poor sister in addition problems until her patience wore thin and with a polite but firm, "Can we do something else now?" she would end it.

I chose a college in rural western Massachusetts, the Berkshire Hill country, and settled down for what I anticipated would be a normal four-year college undergraduate program. I majored in elementary education and minored in music. However, the Lord had His finger in that one, too.

Only one month after school started, I was introduced to Will Hawes by my roommate, Pat. "Don't take him too seriously," she warned, "He's not ready to settle down yet." My happy disposition was not ready to take anyone too seriously. But somehow Will and I hit it off from the very first, and our good solid friendship grew into a strong mutual love. After nearly two and a half years of dating, we were married in 1962. Will was in the U.S. Navy, stationed in San Diego, and I had to return to continue my studies at the University of Massachusetts, a continent away from him. I was able to take my last semester at San Diego State College and transfer my credits back to the University, where I graduated in 1964.

Many of my young-adult friends had never gone along with me in my church activities. They gave two major reasons: some were utterly disillusioned with church leadership or members; others felt that God is somewhere "up in the sky" and cares little about what goes on here on earth. But to me, neither reason made sense. My experience had been with a good God who had healed my mother and blessed our family with good health and prosperity.

Although Mom shared God with me, He became real when Jesus Christ came directly to me in a night vision when I was nine. I had known God as truth, love, peace, joy, and had realized He was everpresent, the intelligence of the universe, and the living substance behind His creation. But these concepts were impersonal. One night Jesus Christ appeared to me, and His love for me streamed from His eyes. Although He spoke no words, His message was crystal clear. He had loved me from the beginning, and He would always love and lead me, as my Lord and Savior. Jesus Christ was *personally* conveying to me His intense love and interest for me alone. I felt that everyone He appeared to must feel the same way. I then knew Him as the active, personal part of the Godhead, whereas God the Father was impersonal. The Lord called me to recognize Him and I felt *called* to His service.

God lived in me and in church. In other words, I found God in every church I attended or served, and I found His Spirit alive in

His people. I taught Sunday school, summer Bible classes, led the junior choir, and made hospital visitations.

I loved Will and I knew him as a child of God. I also knew he would not be receptive to my preaching, so I held my peace and continued to pray for him. When we returned from California we settled into Will's house on the family estate, and I quietly continued my church activities and began to raise our family.

When Betsy was born in 1966 on a balmy May morning, the nurses crowded around to see the beautiful rosy-cheeked baby girl. When Betsy wanted something the whole world knew it! And of course, being the first child to break our quiet family sound barrier, she soon had me well trained to come quickly. Her natural determination was put to good use later on.

Benjamin was born in September 1970. He was as quiet and patient as Betsy was insistent, and the two of them balanced our family nicely. Believing that it was now complete, I projected my energy into several areas. I helped Will's mom bunch carnations for market, played the organ in church and taught piano, and also became involved in church, school, and community activities.

Later, after Mom moved back to Massachusetts and settled next door to us, I helped her with her ministry. It was not surprising or unusual that I should ask for lessons in Christian meditation, since Mom had taught classes and written a book on the subject. She had lectured extensively on many subjects in which I was interested.

CHAPTER FOUR

The Call

Marjorie's independent ministry in a nearby city made the location at the twenty-five acre complex ideal in every way. Peace and harmony reigned, and of the earthly joys, little was lacking. They considered themselves fortunate indeed and believed they were there for the rest of their lives, so comfortable was their setup.

When Linda requested help in meditation, the two of them decided that their meeting time should be early in the morning, before Linda's busy day began. Will had previously attended one series of Marjorie's meditation classes, but had claimed he was not interested in "religious stuff."

Marjorie rose early and would walk through the woods and lawns that separated her house from that of Linda and Will. Together she and Linda would sit at the kitchen table, read the Bible, then pray and meditate. All this was done very quietly so as not to disturb Linda's sleeping family.

One morning about two weeks later, as they were sitting quietly, seeking the Lord's blessing, Linda and Marjorie heard the stairs squeak. A minute later, in walked Will in his robe and slippers, his hair ruffled and his robe crooked.

"What are you two up to?" he queried in a sleepy voice.

"Shush," replied Linda with eyes closed. "Go back to bed. . . . We're meditating."

"Yes," added Marjorie, opening one eye. "You're not interested. Remember? It's not breakfast time yet."

Will slid into the third chair. "Oh well, I'm here. I might as well join you." Then with a note of curiosity, "What do I do?"

They began again, and from that time on, it was a threesome.

They often remarked later how the Lord must have laughed, because here they were, carrying out His very plan, all unknown to them! Simple communion with the Lord was all they sought, but God had bigger plans, only awaiting their humble discovery.

Change usually comes from dissatisfaction or because of difficulties. Change is *usually* forced. Change, however, came to these three out of a cloudless blue!

As noted before, Marjorie's ministry was a comfortable one. Will was in line to take over his parents' wholesale carnation business in a few years and the prospect was pleasing to him and to Linda. It was delightful to work with the flowers, seeing them raised from cuttings and growing to full bloom, ready by the thousands for the Boston Flower Market, of which Will's dad was president. But as they now point out to others, when things become too comfortable, watch out—if you love the Lord—because He is very apt to give you a mighty push out of your cozy nest into new and unexplored fields. And this is exactly what happened to them!

The third month of Bible reading, prayer, and Christian meditation brought their first surprise.

"You are to leave this area. You are to go northward and east," Marjorie intuitively received. Turning to Linda and Will after their meditation, she reported this.

"Oh dear, I don't want to leave here. I wonder if the Lord wants me to go back to Maine?" She had many wonderful friends there, but she didn't enjoy the severe winters and did not look forward to leaving her family and Massachusetts friends behind.

"Maybe I just imagined such guidance," she consoled herself. "We must test our guidance and be sure it comes only from the Lord, Jesus Christ." This they did consistently through consecrated prayer, but time after time, the same message came; it could not be denied.

"Ask the Lord if you are to return to Maine," Linda hesitantly suggested. When Marjorie did, she received, *"No. . . . You are to go to Canada."*

"Canada!" The other two exclaimed. "Why Canada?" But the Lord was adamant. She was to move to Canada. The Lord was dealing with her pleasantly but firmly. *"You promised to go wherever I sent you, after you received your new life. Do you remember?"* He quietly nudged.

"Yes, Lord," she humbly replied. *"Then do as I request,"* He insisted. *"You are to go to a spot of my own choosing—a land you have not seen. The Holy Hand shall guide thee."* A new ministry was about to be born! What more could she ask? Marjorie willingly accepted this beautiful promise.

"Thank you, Lord. I do want only Your will to be done in my life. I will go."

Almost simultaneously, Linda felt the Lord's call in her heart. She had always been close to the Lord and loved to serve Him. This was the climactic call her soul had sought. And Will felt a stirring in his heart. He remembered that when he was five years old, he had the strange feeling that he was on this earth for a special purpose, but he didn't know what it was. He had been wondering about this feeling for years, and at last he had the answer. He was to be a part of this new ministry of Jesus Christ. This was confirmed by the Lord, who said, *"Ye shall go forth together and harvest! Beyond the border of Canada, northward and eastward, lies a city foursquare—magnificent in location, beautiful to behold. Set thy foot upon it, for it is holy ground."*

In giving themselves to the Lord's ministry, they realized they really had nothing to give. Everything they were or ever hoped to be, everything they owned or ever hoped to own, came from His dear hand. He really owned it all, lock, stock and barrel! They dedicated themselves to go where He directed and do whatever they were called upon to do, wherever it might be and whatever sacrifices it might entail.

"Let's ask the Lord more about His perfect plan," Linda insisted. Morning after morning, the three of them received the same guidance—that they were to begin a new ministry together *somewhere* in Canada!

Linda had taken notes on their progress and Marjorie had written down the instructions she had intuitively received from the Lord, Jesus Christ, over the years since His initial communication and ordination calling her to bring His message to the world. This kind of communication is often referred to in our Bible. It is *not* automatic writing from spirits. It is conscious and direct communication with the Lord, Jesus Christ, as described in I Chronicles 28:19: ALL THIS, SAID DAVID, THE LORD MADE ME UNDERSTAND IN WRITING BY HIS HAND UPON ME, EVEN ALL THE WORKS OF THIS PATTERN.

The prophets of old told of the Lord's instructions, which they dutifully wrote down. The prophet Joel, in speaking of the latter days, wrote the word of the Lord: I WILL POUR OUT MY SPIRIT UPON ALL FLESH; AND YOUR SONS AND YOUR DAUGHTERS SHALL PROPHESY, YOUR OLD MEN SHALL DREAM DREAMS, YOUR YOUNG MEN SHALL SEE VISIONS (Joel 2:28).

Those days of which he spoke apparently are here. Many of God's leaders today are doing just these things. Oral Roberts, in *Abundant Life* (October 1983), told that the Lord had spoken to him, giving him directions. Roberts says, "Immediately I reached for a pen and notepad to write down the words as they flooded my inner being."

A similar situation was true for Marjorie. However, she, Linda, and Will would each test the directions separately in prayer. It was obvious that the threesome was receiving an assignment from the Lord that was not immediately complete, but that would gradually unfold to their searching eyes and listening ears, by individual vision and instruction.

It was soon revealed that one of their main jobs was to offer intercessory prayer for the world's people—that they return to God through their Lord and Savior, Jesus Christ—and that others of like mind would join the three to form a prayer community. But how quick the intellect is to deny a divine commission! Like the wandering Israelites being led out of Egypt to the Promised Land, they objected!

"Why can't we pray for people right here at our kitchen table, Lord? Why do we have to move away to do that?"

But the Lord would not be pressured into revealing His whole plan at that time. He proceeded to work patiently with each of them on a personal basis to shape them into the working vessels He had in mind.

21

Week upon week revealed new instructions and visions of what lay ahead. Had they realized the full extent of physical demands before them, they might have been exhausted before they even began! But even as the early Israelites experienced success from obedience, so would the threesome. In faith they clung to the Lord, resolved to STAND FAST THEREFORE IN THE LIBERTY WHEREWITH CHRIST HATH MADE US FREE, AND BE NOT ENTANGLED AGAIN WITH THE YOKE OF BOND-AGE. . . . WHO DID HINDER YOU THAT YE SHOULD NOT OBEY THE TRUTH? (Galatians 5:1,7b).

They were a diversified trio. What one could do well, the other two could hardly do at all. Each fortified and complemented the others. The Lord told them He had chosen them for this special mission not only for this reason, but for the spirit of dedication He had found present in each of them. Linda was musically gifted, a fine composer and arranger, organist and pianist, as well as a trained schoolteacher, church worker, mother, and homemaker. She was a true representative of Love, for as action began to take place in their ministry together, she it was who could always love through a situation and come out victorious!

Will was a typical American man, growing and maturing in the Lord, deeply loving, and talented in mechanics and electrical work. Leaving his engineering major behind, he had graduated in Business Management. He was a true representative of God's Law. He loved it! He found in it the means of self-discipline, human worth, and order. And he found the Lord's grace an amazing, integral part of that law he loved.

Marjorie was a writer, artist, and nature lover; she had experience in building and renovation. She knew the Light of the World first hand. Thus as love, law, and light were represented by the threesome, they were joined in an indissoluble union.

Each of the three was blessed and encouraged amidst the busy schedule of daily living as the Lord commanded, "Claim your inheritance of me and do my good on earth. . . . Come unto me in the mornings of your rests with others of like mind. . . . In the sanctuary . . . seek me and find security." He also told them, "I would have *ye all, in thy own way, come closer unto me . . . so that hour by hour we commune together in whatever task ye do."*

Their Bible confirmed this as they read, WITH MY SOUL HAVE I DESIRED THEE IN THE NIGHT; YEA, WITH MY SPIRIT WITHIN ME WILL I SEEK THEE EARLY: FOR WHEN THY JUDGMENTS ARE IN THE EARTH, THE INHABITANTS OF THE WORLD WILL LEARN RIGHTEOUSNESS (Isaiah 26:9).

"For thy companionship I seek and thy spirit to increase, that in all ways ye may serve with glad and full willing hearts." The Lord often spoke of the "harvest," and they understood He was speaking not only of the crops they would raise, but of the souls they would win for God in the healing prayer ministry that lay ahead of them.

This was a time of great spiritual infilling. One evening during meditation, Linda was blessed by a vision. Perhaps she had been secretly worried about future supply. She saw herself walking northward and east in a heavenly blue light, with the Lord, Jesus Christ, walking beside her. She was on His right. He looked kindly down at her and inquired, *"Linda, who am I?"*

Then he said, *"Remember, I am close enough!"* indicating to her that this was a thought for her to hold, regarding His nature and His tender, loving care. Because He was "close enough," she would always be provided for and have plenty to share with others. She need never fear or worry about going without, when she served her beloved Lord and Master.

Sometimes several days passed without any special word from the Lord, but one morning after such a time, Will was aglow. He reported that during meditation, the Lord had carried him to a beautiful chapel. There were no pews; the focus of attention was upon the altar area. Men dressed in white formed two lines down from the altar, and Will knew he was to stand at the end of the line on the right, although no words were spoken.

It was made known to Will that he was the reason for the gathering. He felt very unworthy. Suddenly a glorious cloud appeared over the altar, and Will knew it was the presence of God. He stepped out of line, walked forward, and knelt, facing the altar.

The hand of God appeared as a beautiful blue-white light, dipped water from a pool, and baptized and anointed him. Will was unable to look up, but he felt the hand of the Lord upon his head, and the warm blessing of ordination. He knew then that he was officially ordained and he began at once to grow beautiful in the Lord.

CHAPTER FIVE

Advance Notice!

As the days passed, the threesome was full of questions. Naturally, they wondered what the country was like where they would be living? They hoped the Lord would give them some kind of preview.

Early one morning, in a vision, the Lord placed Marjorie on a slightly raised mound. Before her spread a rich, fertile, plowed field in a beautiful green valley. A mountain range appeared to rise steeply beyond. Because of her knowledge of nature, she observed the mountain vegetation closely. She noted it was varied, with both evergreen and deciduous trees covering the steep hillsides. This was important—it became a reference point later, as their search unfolded. She sketched the vision for the other two.

"That's interesting," observed Linda, as the three of them examined the drawing. "I wonder if we will have to build a house, or live in a trailer? Perhaps there may be a log cabin available for us to live in." They had two children, plus their dog, Sparkie; and Linda, was naturally concerned about housing.

"Yes!" exclaimed Will. "If I am going to have to build a house, I want to know about it." He hardly knew how to drive a nail, much less frame and build a house! However, the three were filled with a dauntless faith. They knew that the Lord would use the skills they had, and those they did not have, the Lord would surely provide. They were confident that THE LORD'S HAND IS NOT SHORTENED (Isaiah 59:1).

Soon afterward, while they were meditating, the Lord showed Marjorie the house, in which they were to live. It was not the usual farm house. It was brick, a two-story oblong main structure, with a two-story extension. As she looked at the front door, she felt she might be viewing the house from the road and that in their search, if they were not *careful*, they *might* pass by, not seeing it. "We must be sure to look to the left and up, in order to see it," she reported to Linda and Will.

In yet another vision, the Lord showed Marjorie the house again, and this time she saw the two owners—a fairly tall, thin man and a short, robust woman. (These two were to play an important part in working out God's design later on.) The threesome thanked the good Lord as yet another piece of the plan was unfolded to them. This prophecy proved to be 100 percent accurate, as did all those they received.

They were told of the kind people who lived in that locality, and regarding their supply on arrival, the Lord suggested, *"Bank for now your money until that day you leave, for you will need to draw on it for a while."* (They coasted on their bank account for almost nine months.) He spoke also of a barn and fodder for winter use. Cows would not be needed, He told them, but they were to raise *"goats for milk, butter and cheese, sheep for wool and food, fowl for eggs and food."*

Other instructions were given to prepare the little family for a change in living conditions: *"Gather bees to make honey. . . . Cross the border to the north country—a land of waterfalls, rivers and hills and fountains!"* The threesome wondered, what could the Lord mean by "fountains"? They soon guessed there must be springs near the surface in the valley and that there were waterfalls in the mountains nearby, *"as no uncommon sight."* They were stirred to their depths as they tried to imagine the land to which the Lord was sending them.

"Establish my peace through prayer and exposure to my light," the Lord continued. *"Go northward and east. Consider thyself not hindered by events, but blessed by them, for every one who is against me worketh against themselves, though perhaps they know it not!"*

One day a member of Marjorie's congregation casually mentioned a friend of his—a French Canadian—who had invented a new and very clever loom. It was portable and made of lightweight aluminum. Previously, the Lord had told the threesome they would be moving into an area of hand looms and that Linda and Marjorie should begin to acquaint themselves with spinning, dyeing, and weaving, if possible.

At the mention of a loom, Marjorie asked where the inventor lived. It turned out that he lived in Providence, Rhode Island, not too far from their home! Here he manufactured and sold the famous Nadeau Looms and gave instruction in their use. Linda and Marjorie soon made arrangements to pool some funds, buy a loom, and go to Providence weekly for weaving lessons. The members of the Nadeau family became good friends and proved to be experts in their field. Before long Linda and Marjorie were weaving; Linda was especially adept.

Arriving home late one night after driving back from Rhode Island on a long and almost deserted road, Marjorie and Linda parked the car at the back door, entered quietly, and went to bed. The next morning Linda went out to start the car to go to the grocery store. Realizing after a brief time that the car wasn't going to start, she called Will, who efficiently slid behind the wheel and turned the key. The engine turned over perfectly, but the car refused to start.

Puzzled, Will checked everything his born-mechanical mind could think of, then exclaimed in exasperated fashion, "I can't understand why a brand new car won't start! I can't even get a kick or a sputter out of it!" Linda replied that she couldn't understand it either, since it worked like a charm all the way home.

Suddenly Will noticed that the gas gauge read *empty!* The tank was absolutely dry! Had the Lord brought them home without gas, or did it just happen, against all odds, that they arrived at the exact moment the gas was completely gone? Chance or luck? The three-some believed this was another example of the way the good Lord was watching over His little flock. ARE NOT FIVE SPARROWS SOLD FOR TWO FARTHINGS, AND NOT ONE OF THEM IS FORGOTTEN BEFORE GOD? BUT EVEN THE VERY HAIRS OF YOUR HEAD ARE ALL NUMBERED. FEAR NOT THERE-FORE: YE ARE OF MORE VALUE THAN MANY SPARROWS (Luke 12:6-7).

Shortly afterward, a farm extension circular contained the name

27

of a person who knew how to dye wool. This was another exciting learning process for Linda and Marjorie as they experimented with local plant substances. They found Sweet Fern plants in their backyard, which, when brewed, turned their wool a most beautiful golden-yellow color. They learned how to wash the wool in an old washing machine, and this interesting adventure led to the next. Jean, the dyeing instructor, knew someone who could teach them spinning! Hours of happy work evolved as Linda and Marjorie learned the art of hand spinning. During the classes Linda ordered a New Zealand spinning-wheel kit. When it arrived, it was lovingly put aside to take to Canada.

When they had time, all three of them visited local farmers who raised sheep. One, Elsa, told them about sheeps' habits, the best breeds for wool, and rams' butting abilities. Once, she told them, while she was standing with her pet ram in the pasture, she noticed her neighbor across the road waving to her. While she was busy waving back the ram came quietly up behind her, and she found herself sailing over the fence!

It was interesting to watch the Lord preparing them for major changes. At one time, Marjorie was invited to assist at a wedding in a Catholic church. After the ceremony, the guests went to the bride's home for a reception. She was surprised to discover that the bride's parents and most of the guests were of French-Canadian origin. Someone began to play the piano, and soon "O Canada" was being sung with gusto and nostalgia. No one knew at that time of Marjorie's future move, so the song was not deliberately planned, but the tune and words impressed her deeply. Canada, the country that would welcome them in to make their new home, was the sister of her own beloved United States. Gratitude for God's goodness welled up within her as she listened to those good people rejoicing together.

More preparations continued to unfold during morning meditation. One morning in August 1972, the Lord again urged them to *"Cross over the border—go northward and to the east, even as I have directed! Lo, I have pointed the way and shown thee the property . . . in the province that lies beyond the water banks and there to high firm ground."*

They were completely confounded by "the water banks." What on earth could water banks be? None of them could even guess the meaning of the term. They also noted the word "province." At least they were not being sent to the Northwest Territories! However, they were to expect cold weather, and He prepared them for it: *"Complain not if winds be bitter, for it is better to heed my call and come than to stay and be disobedient."* The thought of not obeying His call had never occurred to any of them. Perhaps it was because His call was so clear, so true, and had struck into their very hearts. They loved the Lord and desired to serve Him at any cost. They were to carry the Bible and do justice to it, *"for it is thy staff of life. Make reference to it daily and not be dissuaded by unbelievers who in their hardness of hearts cling to what is theirs rather than to what is mine!"*

Their place was to be a haven of purity and love, where the law of the Lord was respected and obeyed. *"No alcoholic beverage may be used,"* and of course drugs, smoking, and promiscuity were prohibited. Fortunately, the three of them did not smoke or drink or indulge in drugs of any kind, and they were already on their way to medication-free living since in times of sickness, they resorted most often to prayer rather than medication. Had this just "happened," or had the Lord been quietly working with each one to prepare them for His specialized work ahead?

Apparently they were to have crops, for He proceeded to enumerate the products they would raise: *"grains, soy beans, asparagus, onion, fruits, and vines . . . carrot, turnip, vegetables worthy of a good table."* In fact, they were to expect that the land previously had been used for most of these crops, although soy beans and vines would be new.

The instructions were prolific. It became obvious that their farm would be in a valley ringed by low mountains. One day during morning meditation when Marjorie asked, "What does the land look like, dear Lord?" she found herself standing on a knoll of land looking toward the mountains—toward one in particular, which they would own a portion of. The Lord seemed to say abruptly, *"That is EAST!"*—meaning east from the house. Then the Lord's right forefinger appeared, and He traced a capital E in the sky just above "their" mountain.

That precious vision, too, meant that Marjorie should search with compass in hand. What a wonderful Lord, to grant direction in time of need! They praised God and glorified His name as they met each day with awe and reverence.

In considering the purchase of the land, they all wondered how much it would cost. The next day Marjorie was shown the exact amount they were to pay for the property—*"Not a cent more and not a cent less,"* were the instructions. Since they hadn't the vaguest idea where it was located, none of them had any idea whether the amount was even sensible, but they accepted it on pure faith. With the exception of a weekend trip to Quebec City Marjorie and her husband had taken years before, none of them had been in Canada, except for one or two flying trips across the border and back. They had no friends there and little idea of the customs or financial conditions. Only time and circumstances would prove the accuracy of the instructions and prophetic visions they were receiving from the Lord.

Nor were they anxious about gaining entrance to Canada. The Lord assured them they would receive official Canadian residence status before they moved.

CHAPTER SIX

The Search Begins

Interestingly enough, at one time or another, each member of the team was tested by the Lord in three major ways to prove his or her dedication to the cause to which they were being called. The first test concerned money—a test so many fail because of greed or fear. The second test pertained to deliberately doing something wrong and expecting God's protection. The third test had to do with power. God will not allow His power to be misused. As the Bible says, POWER BELONGETH UNTO GOD (Ps. 62:11).

Will's first test came quite unexpectedly when a good friend learned of his decision to go into the ministry and move to Canada. Linda and Marjorie overheard the man's determined voice as he drew Will aside and sincerely tried to convince him that he was making a big mistake. He ended by saying, "Listen, I will give you money—any amount you ask for—if you will reverse your decision." Will responded compassionately; he was not even tempted! True, he did not have much money, but what was money compared to his love for the Lord and his yearning desire to serve Him for the rest of his life? (Later, Will was to meet the other two tests in very interesting ways!)

A similar monetary temptation came to Marjorie. She had inherited property and money from various estates and had been presented with the thought of taking a trip around the world before retiring. True, she loved to travel, but she loved serving the Lord better than anything the world had to offer. Consequently, she invested her inheritance and was now in a good position to help sponsor the Lord's work, even in a new country.

Linda had simple tastes and placed little importance on material possessions, and power tempted none of the three. Their only desire was to do the Lord's will to the very best of their ability. A selfless loyalty to God and to one another developed as the days stretched into weeks, the weeks into months.

As August 1972 came to a close the three were urged by the Lord to *"go in and possess the land which awaits thy possessing!"* They had already received twenty-three prophecies giving the specific prerequisites they needed in order to find the correct property. Five more were to follow. Excitement mounted as they continued to meet each morning, reading the Bible, praying, and sharing the information given them through meditation. Many questions occurred to them: Do you suppose such a place truly exists? Do you believe we will really find it? And if so, how would we ever accomplish the move? It seemed a Herculean task, but no one flinched or backed out! The Lord showed them that their vision was like a seed, that it was to be protected from undue exposure or ridicule. All seeds, even seeds of ideas, need protection, and faith that they will grow. One does not plant a seed, then go out to the garden and dig it up each day to see if it is growing. One plants and waters and has faith that eventually, the seed will develop into a beautiful plant, flowering and bearing seed of its kind. So the vision of the Lord became a precious seed that each of them treasured and protected and blessed.

As September neared, Will reminded them that he had a week's vacation coming. He and Linda suggested that this might be a good time for them all to go to Canada and look around. Marjorie agreed enthusiastically. But where would they begin?

One morning before devotions, Linda eagerly suggested, "Let's ask the Lord to direct us to it, Mom! Let's ask the Lord to draw a map for us."

"Yes," agreed Will, "There's no need to waste time looking. Let's know where we are going!" He had a new station wagon and was eager to try it out.

During the meditation that followed, Marjorie received help by vision and word: *"Lo, I stand and point at the spot where thou goest. Behold where I point."* Before her was an interesting little map with

Quebec City labeled "north"; off to the right, a pyramid with a halo; and an "E" again pointing out East.

"Go hence, seek and ye shall locate that which is for you!" Then the Lord added a real bonus—*"Lo, I go before you preparing the way, and I ease the strain for thee!"* What strain? They couldn't imagine any strain as they sat comfortably in Massachusetts that warm autumn day.

Linda took the little map Marjorie had drawn from the vision the Lord had given her, and laid it on the large map. "There's Quebec City," she announced. "And look, it's almost exactly north of where we are! The Lord said for us to go northward and east. Remember?"

Carefully scrutinizing the map and the drawing, Will placed a cautious finger on the Gaspé. "I figure the place must be somewhere near here," he surmised. Marjorie looked over his shoulder as Linda applied a magnifying glass to the area.

"I doubt that," Marjorie enjoined. "The Lord wouldn't send us to a place none of us have even visited! None of us have ever been near that part of the country in our lives!"

Will sat back and stared at her. "Now, what makes you think He would not send us to some place we have never been?" he inquired. "The Lord is full of surprises—take us, for instance!"

"Well," interrupted Linda brightly, "how about New Brunswick? That's near us. A friend of mine said the land was beautiful when she was up there a few years ago—nice and fertile, like the Lord told us!"

"But the Lord also said it was beyond the water banks," added Marjorie thoughtfully. "Now that sounds to me like it might be north of the St. Lawrence River. There must be some water banks there. It's a big, deep river."

"Northward and east leads us to the Gaspé Peninsula," Will insisted.

"I doubt that," Marjorie interrupted. "I remember way back in fifth-grade geography, there was a picture of a poor Gaspésian farmer standing and looking down at his plowed field, and it was loaded with big rocks—awful soil! The land the Lord showed me was beautiful rich soil, and I didn't notice any huge rocks in it—small ones maybe, but the land was fertile! God would never send us to the Gaspé!"

"Well, that's where it looks to me like it is," replied Will.

"Yes," chimed in Linda. "It could very well be there, Mom. Look!" She pointed again from Quebec City to the Gaspé on a line east from the city. "Although you may be right," Linda hesitated. "Why don't we drive directly to Quebec City and go on from there?"

"I still think it's on the Gaspé," Will muttered, "but if you two are determined to drive north of the St. Lawrence, I guess I'm outnumbered. At least I've got my dog." Sparkie came over and nuzzled him affectionately.

Previously, the Lord had told them to locate the property in the fall, make a deposit on it, and complete the transaction in the spring when they moved in. Of course, He knew the people wanted to sell in the fall and move out in the spring! He also knew lots more He wasn't telling the threesome!

And so it was settled: They would leave shortly and drive directly to Quebec City, pray, and try to find their way from there. The family proceeded to decide what to take—a tent, camp stove, utensils, food, sleeping bags and cots in case they were caught out somewhere, and clothes. Thus the Dodge was loaded, and the three adults, the children, and the dog climbed in.

On the morning of August 28, 1972, their car crawled out of the yard on the first lap of an adventurous one-week search. The sun was shining, the air was fresh, and they were eager with anticipation, expecting to locate their future home quickly and easily.

The distance to Quebec City, some three hundred fifty miles, was covered with Will at the wheel most of the time and Marjorie and Linda substituting at intervals. After a good night's rest they went directly to the Touriste Information booth, where they were met with all kinds of literature to help them "Découvrer la Belle Provence!" Much of the literature was in French. Although they all had taken it in high school or college, the speech was more rapid and different from the Parisian French they had been taught years ago. However, there was sufficient help by English-speaking tour guides, and a great deal of English literature also was available.

They eagerly took the bulletins that contained pictures and scanned them carefully, trying to find country that matched what the Lord had shown them. Nothing looked familiar—winding waterways, covered bridges, snowmobile and ski resorts, wayside shrines, parks, trails, chalets and log cabins, massive churches and covered archways, open fields, mountain forests, art treasures— and, of course, pictures of the beautiful dazzlingly blue water of the St. Lawrence and the open Atlantic. They could not find one single clue to help them!

Countryside

They gasped when they were told that the government parks and preserves, in the main forests of the province of Quebec alone, covered an area twice as large as the country of Portugal! This largest of all the provinces was bounded on the north by the Hudson Strait, on the east by Labrador, on the south by New Brunswick, and on the west by Ontario. Its territory also included

Anticosti and the Magdalen Islands, but the threesome was not interested in such far-reaching. Most of Quebec's six million people had settled in the Montreal and Quebec City areas, with about a quarter of the population in scattered rural areas, leaving large portions of the province as wilderness too forsaken and dangerous for anyone to inhabit. Looking at the awesome maps of the province, they began to wonder whether they had a tiger by the tail—and if so, what to do with it!

Since the Lord had told them to enjoy exploring their new environment and become acquainted with it, they decided to begin with the city of Quebec. The pronounced influence of Indian heritage, as well as French and English, fascinated them—especially when they learned that the Indians had probably originally migrated from Asia by way of the Aleutian Straits into Alaska, then worked their way east, developing the cultivation of corn, potatoes, and tobacco; inventing canoes and snowshoes—all necessities of life in the great Canadian north.

The three refreshed their long-forgotten history as they scanned the travel folders. In 1535 Jacques Cartier, the famous French explorer, had discovered the Baie des Chaleurs south of the Gaspé Peninsula. He took possession of the land in the name of France and went up the Restigouche River, returning to St.-Martin cove, which is now Port Daniel. From there he went to Cape Pratto (Percé, site of the famous rock), then up the river which he named the Saint Laurent (Saint Lawrence) to Kebec (Quebec City), and on to Hochelaga (now called Montreal). Later Champlain founded a settlement in Kebec, but the winter was so rigorous only eight of the original twenty-eight settlers survived.

Although in previous centuries a succession of explorers—Vikings, Basques, and Portuguese—had come to this land Cartier called New France, they had never permanently colonized it. In 1759 the English General Wolfe defeated the French General Montcalm on the Plains of Abraham (near Quebec City), and in 1763 the Treaty of Paris was signed, giving the English ruling rights to the country.

Today Quebec City, the capital of the Canadian province of Quebec and the only walled city in North America, rises from a huge mass of rock with fortifications around the Citadel, giving it a powerful military command of both land and water approaches to the city. The family viewed the historic city gates, still standing as a memento of early days, and once the only means of entering or leaving the fortress city. The shaded, tree-lined, flowered streets gave the impression of a charming European community in the Middle Ages.

The city is divided into two parts—the lower or original city and the upper, newer part. The old lower city, with its narrow cobblestone streets, had no sidewalks, but the inhabitants had built covered bridges between the houses. Betsy delightedly hopped along the cobblestones as Ben laughed at her antics. In the upper part of the city were broad avenues and beautiful residences as well as the famous Chateau Frontenac. There was much to see and do.

Drawing to one side after a ride in a horse-drawn open carriage, the family prayed and compared notes. Which direction should they take from here? They decided to go east, following the main highway that skirted the wide St. Lawrence River. To the east lay hundreds of miles of territory they had yet to explore. The map showed the road ending at Sept-Iles, four hundred miles to the northeast.

Because the Lord had told them *their* place was in a valley bordered by mountains, as they drove along the coast they explored many roads that led to the left, inland, thoroughly following the trails to their very end. They were serious and did not intend to miss the blessing their Lord had promised them! As they traveled, they enjoyed the scenery, read the Bible aloud, prayed, and sang praises to God, and they were comforted by feeling the Lord's presence in their midst.

At the famous shrine of Ste. Anne de Beaupré, they all got out of the car and stretched their legs. Sparkie ran after the children as they tried to catch a late butterfly, and the threesome studied their list of prerequisites. This was a wonderful time to ask the blessing of the Lord on the list and rededicate themselves to doing their level best to obey their Lord's instructions.

The season for pilgrim visits to the holy shrine had tapered off.

There would be another celebration in October on Canadian Thanksgiving Day, and the Christmas festivities after that. They had missed the evening candlelight processions, the marches of penitents, the hymn singing. Many of the two million pilgrims that year had come and gone. Ste. Anne's spring bubbled quietly, awaiting its next healing candidate.

Along the hillside could be seen the stations on the Way of the Cross with its bronze-covered statues from France. There was an aura of peace over the silver granite basilica, rarely used for religious ceremonies; rather, it was a place of prayer to pay homage to the mother of the Blessed Virgin, Mary, and to give thanks for the wonderful miracles in that corner of North America.

Legend tells that sailors from Breton who came up the St. Lawrence in 1650 were caught in a terrible storm and almost shipwrecked. But they vowed that if their lives were spared they would build a chapel at that point to honor Ste. Anne, their patroness, and they were saved. History tells us that in that same year the first land grants were made, and eight years later the first little wooden chapel was erected as promised. During its construction a miraculous healing took place, and other miracles continued over the years that followed.

Before the family left Ste. Anne de Beaupré they drove up the road, zigzagging between the twenty-eight-step Scala Santa and the Franciscan convent to the top of a ridge, where a magnificent view of the town and the great river with its islands, was spread out before them.

As they drove on, two miles beyond the paper-mill community of Beaupré the paved road to St. Fereol provided access to the Parc du Mont-Ste. Anne. The summit of its notable mountain, over 2,600 feet high, towered above valleys of scenic beauty. But no part of the territory appeared to match the careful descriptions of "their" place given them by the Lord.

Highway 15 climbed over the mountains of Les Caps through lovely forests of young spruce. Panoramic views met them at every turn of the mountainous journey. Majestic ocean liners, cruising up the river to the ports awaiting them, looked like tiny toys in a sea of blue. A few houses were scattered along the way as they ventured off on side roads bearing north or east. These inevitably led to passages through wilderness territory, between mountains or over them into uninhabited lands, whereupon they would turn around and retrace their route.

They passed through a tiny hamlet farther on where a mountain stream rushed down into a picturesque gorge bordered by shrubs and wildflowers with blooms quite different from any they had seen before. Venturing off the beaten highway was certainly an adventure in itself! They eventually stopped for the night in the little village of Ste. Tete des Caps, at a clean and comfortable motel.

CHAPTER SEVEN

New Discoveries

The next day dawned bright, clear, and full of hope! After breakfast the family got underway again. The country was new to all of them: scenic rolling hills, winding roads with lovely views from every height—and lots of dust—as they made their way into the wilderness, to the very end of every gravel road. As they passed through St. Placide, each set of eyes was watching, hoping to find some familiar landmark given them by the Lord. But none was to be seen. Most of the trees were deciduous, the landscape was not at all like that they had been shown. They pressed on, hoping the next mile might reveal a change that would fit the picture.

As the day passed and night began to fall, motels became fewer and farther apart. It was late, Will was cross, the children were restless, and all their nerves were wearing thin when at last a rather second-rate motel appeared. They stopped and Will got out to inquire if there was room. Yes, there were vacancies! They told him the price and he looked at two adjoining rooms. The facilities were old and the linen doubtful, but Will went back into the office anyway to pay the bill. The price immediately went up! That was all Will needed to convince him this was not the place for them! So they drove off into the night, their empty tummies growling, not knowing where they would find food or their next resting place.

That was the night when, after driving for miles, Will suddenly spotted the wood road and turned into it. That was the gala night of the black flies! And that was the first night they spent in the tent. The lesson for the day was—*"Cease your murmurs and rejoice and be glad—you must learn to love more!"* Had they been murmuring? They were learning to work in harmony and love—a mighty lesson for three! Love more people, love more situations, love more conditions and circumstances. *"Love is the answer."*

The field was moist with dew as the sun rose to greet the travelers after they had faithfully held morning prayers in the tent. Again they studied their map and found they were high in the interior of Quebec, across from Chicoutimi, on the other side of the river Saguenay that flowed out of the large Lac St. Jean. They decided that after breakfast they would head down a long dirt road through the Parc de Chicoutimi to Tadoussac, on the main highway, Route 138, which followed the St. Lawrence River east.

As they opened the tent door, they were greeted by others who wanted breakfast also! Not only were black flies present, but hordes of mosquitoes had received the message in the night and arrived for a morning feast! Linda cooked breakfast on one well-bitten leg and scratched it with the other, slapping her hair and neck to drive off the ravenous creatures. Will raced through the underbrush, crashing like an elephant, pulling up the tent stakes and folding up the tent as quickly as possible, with the help of Marjorie and the children. Breakfast was gulped down hungrily, the utensils gathered quickly, and everyone piled into the car, rolled up the windows, and breathed a sigh of relief. Ah! The haven of an automobile!

"I suspect that when Henry Ford developed his cars, he never thought of this use for them," commented Will as he gleefully squashed the last mosquito and removed the last of the black flies from the windshield with the wipers. (How hard it is to learn to love those that sting us!)

The road ahead was undeveloped, narrow, winding hardpan—and dusty, as was the road over which they had come. They went very slowly and carefully, lest a car from the other direction meet them on a sudden curve or downhill grade. It took a long time to return to the paved main highway and head northeast again.

A little farther on, they came to Les Escoumins. Here another road wound off to the left.

"We had better follow it," Linda advised. "It may just lead to the valley and mountains we are looking for!"

This gravel road took a precarious route along the steeply banked Escoumins River amidst dense evergreen forests. It had been quite some time since they had seen any houses, when suddenly they came upon a road crew that had just finished building a bridge across a rushing stream. Waving good naturedly, the Canadians graciously stepped aside to let them pass. They doubtless wondered what a car from Massachusetts was doing way up there!

They continued for miles into the interior without sight or sound of habitation. Passing several lakes, they finally came to a halt at Lac Lorrey when the road they were following continued no farther. There they turned around and followed a scenic river route, with bending trees mirroring their greenery in the water below, back to the main highway.

Breathing a prayer of thanksgiving, the little party, still traveling east, continued on the main highway through Sault au Mouton toward Forestville. Following another road that led off to the left, they found that it became narrower and narrower and finally ended in a maze of wood roads leading in different directions. Some of these were fire roads and some were logging trails, but the threesome did not know that. Choosing one, they had bumped along for some distance when another intersection presented itself. Then another and another. Soon they were lost—lost in the Canadian wilderness with the gas gauge low!

"What shall we do?" The panic button seemed ready to sound.

"Pray!" advised Marjorie. And pray they did! Will turned around and headed back, but the roads led in confusing directions. They prayed at each crossroad, and because they refused to fear, the Lord was able to show them where a road grader had passed, and they followed a smoother road back to civilization.

As they neared Forestville, all the family members discussed the things they were learning. It was a many-faceted search and each was making individual discoveries. The children chattered excitedly together on the back seat, with Sparkie between them.

"Remember the eagle's nest we saw, Bennie?" Betsy exclaimed. "It was way up high and made of lots of sticks and things!" Ben grinned amiably.

The grownups also exchanged notes. Their talk was not the usual discussion of scenery, industry, and people, but rather the soul lessons they were learning: patience, self-control, tolerance for one another's differences, kindness and understanding. It was indeed a precious trip with the Lord's Holy Spirit active as a catalyst in their midst.

Arriving at Forestville, they discovered a city that had revived only thirty years before, having gone to sleep in 1890. The exploitation of forest resources had brought it back to life and industry now flourished. Water was used to float the logs downstream, where a unique method of loading the pulpwood was practiced: Streams of water from pumps forced the logs onto a conveyor. The family got out to look. Sparkie and the children ran and played while the grownups talked with the lumbermen.

Regathering and climbing into the car, they again followed a gravel side road. This one led up into the mountain range. Here the trees seemed smaller and thinner, and rocky crags pointed towering fingers toward the sky as the river tumbled below. The road led inland and it was getting dark. Pulling into a level clearing, Will turned off the motor.

"Let's camp here for the night," he suggested. Everyone thought that was a good idea, since they could still see sufficiently well to set up the tent and cook.

Soon the aroma of beans and toast filled the air. Milk from the cooler, brown bread, and pickles, and their supper was set on a tablecloth on the ground. The fragrance of the cedar forest blended with the clean smell of the earth and the mountain air. With everyone helping out, they were all soon happy to have prayers and settle down in their tent for a deep night's sleep. The calls of the owls or the howl of an occasional bobcat did not keep them awake that night! The only thing Marjorie remembered was that Will's knees occasionally scraped her back as he turned over on the bunk cot beneath her. Linda rested close beside him, with Betsy on a cot beside her. Ben lay sprawled in his sleeping bag at their feet— and Sparkie guarded the door, but he also was tired and slept.

The next morning after devotions and breakfast, they again loaded the car and set off up the road to an unknown destination. They had not picked up any leaflets with information about that particular area, so they traveled slowly and carefully. An hour had passed without event when suddenly Will leaned forward and squinted.

"Well, what do you know!" he muttered. There up ahead was a bleak cabin—and yet more cabins! In fact, there was a whole sea of cabins, most of them empty, but some with real live people in them!

"Signs of habitation," Marjorie observed. " I wonder where we are."

"Let's ask," Linda suggested.

"Look! A man!" Ben ventured, pointing to someone walking in their direction.

"Yes, and he's got a dog with him, see?" added Betsy.

Will drove up to the man. "Where are we?" he inquired.

"Labrieville," the man replied. He pointed up ahead and there at a distance, towering in the sun, was a huge bare mountainside that looked at least a thousand feet high—straight up! Up on the sheer cliff was a single man, climbing a ladder to a top lost in foliage. They got out of the car and watched him in awe.

Without realizing it, they had arrived at what was known as Bersimis I. Bersimis I is a huge hydroelectric plant. A few miles to the north, immense dams confined the waters of the Bersimis River, known as "the great whirlpool" because of its size and tumultuous power. The generating plant, literally built in the living rock of the mountain, was fed from a man-made reservoir covering three hundred square miles. The waters were conducted to the plant through a tunnel seven and one-half miles long, also hollowed out of living rock.

They were told that twenty miles downstream, another dam, Bersimis II, produced horsepower in a more conventional manner, and the energy was eventually delivered to Montreal and other parts of the province by Hydro-Quebec. Immense transmission lines with towering pylons carried the power to its destination. Workmen told them that Bersimis I was then producing over one million horsepower and Bersimis II, over 900,000 horsepower. It was an impressive sight.

However, the countryside resembled not at all what they were looking for, and although each place was interesing and could have provided many hours of exploration, there was no point in pursuing those projects further. The gravel road made slow driving necessary, lest a rock fly up and damage the transmission or knock a hole in the gas tank. The fifty miles back to the main highway seemed like a long way, but they eventually arrived and then continued northeast through Colombier, Ilets Jeremie, Betsiamites, Ragueneau, and on to another fairly new city, Hauterive.

Hauterive was located along the estuary of the mighty Manicougan and St. Lawrence rivers. Established in 1950, the place now boasted some 12,000 residents, most of whom were involved in the prosperous commerce that had formed around the world's largest hydroelectric development at that time. The Manicougan and Chute Aux Outardes projects were still under construction and Manic I Powerhouse was located within the town limits.

Observing the now quiet waters of the Manicougan, the visitors did not realize it had been harnessed farther north by the McCormick dams and had, by that time, produced millions of horsepower. An airport enabled workers and visitors to fly to the city directly from Montreal.

Six miles east of Hauterive, the travelers entered Baie Comeau. Here an exciting city had been created by men of vision and courage, in an isolated area not then linked with the civilized world by overland communication. Colonel Robert McCormick, publisher of the *Chicago Tribune,* is said to have inspired a handful of construction engineers and paper specialists to establish a pulp and newsprint mill there in 1936. A large waterfall supplies a hydroelectric station which generates power for the paper mill. The water was brought from a dam to the generating station by a conduit built out of British Columbian pine, the longest wooden pipe of its type in the world.

As the town developed, two other commercial ventures took root—a large aluminum refinery in 1958, and huge grain elevators two years later. Because of its natural deep-water port the industries are able to ship their products to world centers year-round, since the Atlantic waters at that point are seldom blocked by ice. A municipal airport serves the region, and sportsmen are flown into the interior to try their luck with speckled trout and salmon.

45

The threesome found this town extremely interesting. Built on the slopes of rocky outcroppings, it overlooks the bay, providing charming vistas. Here their feeling of being in frontier country was even more intense! Although it was a sizable town at that time, it still had an air of newness, of unfamiliarity with its environment, as if it had just settled onto the ground.

Baie Comeau may have seemed near the end of the world to the family, but it was like any other Canadian or U.S. town on Labor Day! Everyone and everyone's cousin had come in to celebrate! They came from the forests and mines, from ships and farms and fisheries, for this was a great port as well as an industrial center. The town rocked on its heels. Unshaven men in high boots, girls in skimpy dresses, careworn couples with their children, singles— everyone, it seemed, was looking for pleasure and everyone needed a place to spend the night.

It was only through prayer and great diligence that our travelers finally located a motel that would give them one room with two single beds. No rollaways were available. The motel stood on the edge of a loose landfill of boulders and gravel covered with underbrush. But at that late hour the location was unimportant. They had been trained by the Lord to be grateful and give thanks for every blessing that came their way.

Weary from their long journey, they made no effort to unpack, but fell sleepily into bed. During the night, each adult took a turn sleeping on the floor. It was cold and drafty, but they were grateful. God was good! Besides, every day thus far had been sunny!

Rising early the next morning, they shook the wrinkles out of their clothing, prayed, read the Bible aloud as usual, meditated upon it, and then listened to Jesus Christ for their daily instruction. *"Follow through on the project. Even though thou failest in some respects, in others thou shalt win!"* This was encouraging news! The rest of the message led them to wonder where on earth they were going! *"Go north and thus complete thy mission thus far. Carefully contemplate the past way."*

So they continued north, past many coves and fishing villages, still exploring each gravel road that led off the main highway in the hope of finding their valley home in the mountains. As the landscape became more and more rugged and the vegetation took on a windswept appearance, the scenic village of Godbout came into view. Godbout sported an unusual industry—a periwinkle cannery—as well as a ferry service across the St. Lawrence River to the Gaspé Peninsula.

Originally a fur trading post, Godbout still had an excellent salmon river, and there was a lovely beach. An old Indian cemetery held a large mausoleum erected in the memory of one of the most illustrious sons of the North Shore, the famous naturalist Napoleon Alexandre Comeau, who died in 1923. A tablet paid tribute to this naturalist, hunter, physician, and saver of lives, "The humble child of the North," who spent the last sixty years of his life in Godbout.

As the car followed the shore road, its passengers eagerly scanned the St. Lawrence, hoping to see the ferryboat, but it was nowhere in sight. Passing the ferry landing, the threesome determined to continue their search to the very end! They arrived at Port Cartier, once a spot in the wilderness marked on a map by explorer Cartier, now a busy little port of trade. To the north stretched a dirt road that followed a railroad. The map showed that the roadway soon dwindled out, but the railway continued miles onward, eventually ending at the mining community of Gagnon in the Quebec northern wilderness. No towns appeared on the map for the almost two hundred miles between Port Cartier and Gagnon. The threesome were learning about the vast spaces of Canada!

As they traveled up the seacoast, twenty-five miles beyond the Port they came to Sept-Iles, so named because of the seven islands off its shore. The sheltered harbor lent refuge to ships coming in from the open sea, the seven islands serving as natural jetties. Here they saw another railroad track that wandered north into Labrador and, after hundreds of uninhabited miles, ended in a mining community known as Schefferville. According to their map, this was the northernmost section of railway in eastern North America.

Following the main highway as far as it went, Linda, Will, and Marjorie discovered that fifteen miles out of Sept-Iles, the pavement dwindled off into a cart path. They were near the border of Labrador!

A ferry at Sept-Iles could take them by water to various fishing coves along the coast, or south to the northern shore of the Gaspé Peninsula! Horseback and jeep were the only means of land transportation. They had gone as far east as they could go! Beyond the end of the main highway lay Ha Ha Bay (Indian, something pleasant or confusing).

"This is one name we can all pronounce!" Linda laughed. It was obvious this was not the country the Lord had directed them to, but they appreciated the education they had received from visiting this beautiful, unspoiled land. They hastily turned around and headed back the way they had come.

CHAPTER EIGHT

The Gaspé

They had done a thorough job of combing the countryside. They had found no house identical to their vision, no long fertile valley bordered by mountains, no noticeable water banks, and the forests appeared to be all deciduous or all evergreen or sparse vegetation— nothing fitted the descriptions so carefully given them by their Lord, Jesus Christ. They felt they were right in having come that far and in becoming acquainted with the province and her people, but now they were ready to explore other areas. They weren't about to give up, even though Will's vacation time was running out.

Driving the ninety or so miles back to Godbout, they felt guided to take the ferry across to Matane on the northern shore of the Gaspé Peninsula, since it would be a more direct route home than returning the long way through Quebec City. In fact, they would not have time to get home if they took the long way.

The children were delighted at the prospect of a ferryboat ride! They had been very good all the way, playing games, looking at the scenery, and taking part in any action that came along. The radio had not been on so that the group could concentrate on God's will and succeed in their mission. When they reached the ferry, a long line of cars—tourists with their souvenirs, trappers, fishermen in high boots, tradesmen and pedestrians noisily filed on board. After they were underway, passengers wandered about the deck and groups of children ran up and down stairs. Some of the people in the cabin kept going out to look anxiously at the sky. It had been overcast since the beginning of the crossing and rain began to fall in sheets as the ferry unloaded its passengers, both cargo and cars, at Matane. This was the first rain they had encountered on the trip.

The city of Matane was a lumber and salmon-fishing center. None of the three had ever set foot on Gaspé land before. They had seen some of the north shore of the St. Lawrence, now they were about to see some of the south shore. Perhaps their place was below Quebec in New Brunswick, and they would find it on the way home.

A beautiful motel with a restaurant came into view. There was one large room available, and it was clean and comfortable—a wonderful place to eat, clean up, wash clothes, and have Bible reading, prayers, and meditation before going to bed.

When they awoke the next morning it was still raining and blowing. "What do You want us to do today?" they questioned as they prayed and meditated on God's will.

They received, *"Tarry till the storm is past. . . . Learn all thou canst about the land in which thou shalt dwell. Pray. Read your Bible and be quiet listeners today."* And so that day was a quiet, restful, prayer-filled, Bible-reading day—a wonderful day again with the Lord. The children read, played in the recreation room, and ran in the open porch around the motel.

In the afternoon the storm abated and the temperature became warmer, almost as though spring had come again. Marjorie and Betsy decided to take a short walk. A strange little furry animal followed them back to the motel. It was a cute little ball of fluff, different from anything they had seen before. It came so close to them they ran for shelter, not knowing what it was or whether it might bite.

When a motel workman rounded the corner with mop and cleaning tools, the tiny animal ran through an open door into an empty room and under the bed. Looking at them the man inquired, in French, "Is this yours?" Marjorie and Betsy looked at each other and Betsy giggled. If they said no, he might kill it. But they did not want to lie, so they just shrugged and smiled. He assumed the animal was their pet, so he kindly went in and drove the creature out with a broom. It ran up to Marjorie and Betsy and, sitting on its haunches, chattered a little speech, almost as though saying "Thank you for sparing my life," and then it ran off.

They have wondered since what kind of animal it could have been. It was about the size of a weasel or mink, but more cuddly and very friendly. It did not seem to fit the description of any creature they had seen in animal books.

It had been a day of rest. They had "worked" industriously the previous days, so how good of the Lord to instruct them now to rest and pray. As the day drew to a close, the three suddenly realized that it was their seventh day on the road, and of course they should have a Sabbath. Unbeknown to them, the Lord had led them into this Sabbath day of rest.

When the family went to dinner, the English-speaking waitress asked if they had had a good day. As they responded joyfully, she added, "It is good you stayed, because of the hurricane! It is almost over now." Hurricane? They had not heard about a hurricane, since they had not watched television or had the radio on. The Lord had previously told them they did not need news from outside sources in order to be protected, *if* they listened to Him and obeyed Him. They simply followed God's guidance and had been perfectly protected. God was SO good!

That evening each person listed the blessings he or she had received from the Lord thus far on the trip. The children's lists were especially sweet. Betsy wrote, "I am grateful for the beautiful sea, rocks, hills, little clean brooks and their waves." After Betsy read her list out loud, Ben said, "Me too!"

The next morning in Matane dawned crystal bright. They were disappointed about returning home without having found their place of ministry, but when they spoke to the Lord about it, He assured them, *"Man was made for reaching."* What a beautiful thought! (Later Linda wrote a song on that theme.) Then the Lord added, *"Go forward to victory! Behold, my Spirit goeth before you to make your way pleasant and agreeable. You are meeting your tests well. . . . . Prove thyselves capable, competent workers."*

Then He gave them some instruction that was to last the rest of their lives: *"Do not neglect the little decencies of the day, but be too generous rather than too skimpy — too understanding rather than too domineering, too tender rather than hard-hearted. . . . Go forth, I say, into the dawning of a new day and rejoice!"*

It was not difficult for them to "go forth" that day—a day that dazzled with fresh-washed brightness. But should they go east or west, or perhaps south through the center of the peninsula? On the map, they had noticed a dirt road that wound from the north shore, where the Gaspé Peninsula bordered the St. Lawrence, to the south shore and the salt-water Baie des Chaleurs.

Through meditation, they all received the same impression— that they were to go east along the St. Lawrence for a while, and then take the road south. In this way they would make the best possible use of their time in order to see the country.

Children, adults, and dog piled into the car, and off they drove toward the end of the thick tongue of land, some 175 miles long, if measured through the center, and about 90 miles wide. Studying the guidebook, Linda read that the Indians had originally named the peninsula Gaspeg, meaning Land's End.

Route 6 (now Route 132), following the circumference of the peninsula, is a 400-mile trail along sandy beaches or on the edge of high plateaus that occasionally dropped as sheer cliffs into the sea. Heavily wooded, and well populated by the Micmac Indians in the early days, the peninsula is formed around some of the highest mountains in eastern Canada, dominated by the Jacques Cartier, some 4,300 feet high. The Indians called these the Chic-Chocs, or Rocky Mountains—volcanic formations with denuded summits. The Gaspé Peninsula is hundreds of millions of years old, one of the oldest lands on earth.

Again the travelers carefully studied the information booklets they had picked up in Quebec City, but still could not find anything similar to their visions. At Ste. Anne des Monts they turned right. The dirt road that led south was only ninety miles long, but seemed longer because of its condition. It cut through the Parc de la Gaspésie (with camping accommodations), wound through a corner of the Parc de la Petite Cascapedia, skirted mountains, and followed wild, rushing streams through deep gorges. The scenery was breathtaking!

Their yellow station wagon was by now so covered with dust that no color showed. Dust not only was on the outside, but inside as well. They drove in, sat in, lived in, and ate dust, yet were surrounded by the glory of God's magnificent countryside. However, with the millions of miles of highways Canada needed to keep up, they were grateful for roads that were even passable.

After driving fifty miles through the deserted park, they met one lonely car—a car with a flat tire! They stopped in the middle of the road and Will got out to see if they could help. Then suddenly, two more automobiles appeared, one coming from either direction, so that Will had to return and move their car. Those were the only other vehicles they saw on their entire ninety-mile trip through the park.

Returning to the disabled car, they learned that the spare was flat also, and the driver needed a ride to the nearest garage—wherever that might be.

The man climbed in with Will, while Linda, Marjorie, and the children remained with the man's wife. The men drove forty miles to Cascapedia, where a mechanic pumped up the spare, and then returned to their families. Needless to say, the couple was very grateful and the threesome felt rewarded, knowing they had been able to help someone in need. They continued toward Cascapedia, on the south shore of the Gaspé, then turned right, heading home.

Will's vacation was now over. He had called home and received one extra day, but he felt pressed to return. Driving along the salt water of the Baie des Chaleurs (Body of Heated Waters), they arrived at a little town called Maria. There was a long, inviting beach, clean and beautiful, and the family was tempted by the clear blue crystal waters.

There was also a Micmac Indian reservation at Maria. A gift shop and a wooden Roman Catholic church, both shaped like huge teepees caught their attention. Stopping at the gift shop, they found the Indians making baskets and snowshoes and other hand-crafted items which they sold on the spot. The teepee was a unique way to attract the tourist trade.

As evening approached, the family saw a small motel village that looked so appealing they decided to stay there for the night. This turned out to be an important decision. They rented a log cabin on the shore and enjoyed a walk by the water before they went inside for devotions and a good night's rest.

During this night, the Lord, Jesus Christ gave Linda a very significant vision. In fact, He gave her clearly defined directions to lead her right to the place they were searching for! She woke everyone early the next morning to share the exciting news. At last, they could drive to their place and arrange to buy it—they would not have to go back home empty-handed!

CHAPTER NINE

The Search Continues

Linda carefully explained her vision. She saw "Main Street," which she interpreted to mean the main route (Route 6). She saw them driving east (reversing their direction from their return home), until they came to a Post Office. It was a small brick Post Office, on the right side of the road. They were to turn left onto a road that led up into a valley between the mountains.

"And," she added, "the Lord said there would be a river near the road that would bound our property, but *we would not be able to see it!* Can you imagine a river beside the road and not being able to see it??" They all considered this.

"Perhaps it runs underground at that point," Will suggested.

"Maybe there is dense foliage along the road that conceals it," guessed Marjorie. Speculate as they might, none of them discerned the real reason the river was not visible, so near the road.

Without losing further time, they had devotions, ate a hasty breakfast, and asked the Lord what they should do about Linda's vision. He replied, " *'Main Street' signified by main highway off of which ye turn and follow the land by the water, northward, and here in the valley ye shall find."* What could be easier than that?

Then He added, *"Follow the leading of the Holy Spirit within and go forward to victory! The land is yours, even as I have shown you. Look in the spots I direct and ye shall find. Each one within himself has my word."*

"Believe that with God all things are possible. . . . Did I not rise from the dead and ascend so that my Spirit could be present with you whithersoever ye go? . . . Enjoy thy day!"

Indeed they would enjoy this day of all days! Praying and singing

55

their thanks to God and without further delay, they set off. They all sat on the edge of their seats, with Linda excitedly pointing the way. They passed through New Richmond, an English settlement, then on to Black Cape, where a large Roman Catholic retreat house sat perched on a scenic point of land overlooking the beautiful Baie, on through Caplan. Farming, fishing, and lumbering operations showed clearly the extent of the people's industry. They were wholesome, happy, simple folk, contented to live off the land and the sea, and devoted to God and to their families. The sapphire waters sparkled beautifully in the sun.

On they drove, through St. Simeon and Bonaventure, passing an occasional artist trying to capture the scenic beauty with oils and canvas. The seaport town of Bonaventure, settled by the French, had been burned by Commodore Lord Byron, the grandfather of the celebrated poet. In 1760 the first twelve French Acadian families had settled there after fleeing from the British in Nova Scotia, and one of their little wooden houses still remained. But where was the brick Post Office? Where was the valley opposite it? Where was the valley road leading north? With all the directions they had been given, not one was being evidenced!

True, they had passed several brick Post Offices, but they were all on the left, or else the valley and road description did not match. Many disappointing miles later, they came to a halt in a shopping center and Marjorie sought out a clump of bushes to be alone to commune with the Lord and seek His direction, while Will and Linda prayed with her in the car. Will was shaken. Linda received that Will should call home and ask for more time off so that they could find the place, now that they were so close.

Marjorie shared what she received. *"Have I not said it takes strong faith to serve? This is a test wherein ye meet the difficulties and overcome them by the truth. . . . Will ye meet them if ye wilt at every discouragement? I have called thee out from among them. . . . Look not back, but forward. . . . Pick thyself up and go on with gladness of heart that thou art privileged at this time and chosen for my holy purpose. Those I find unworthy are they who falter and fade from purpose. Keep steady and faith-filled and all shall be well. . . . Come unto the valleys and mountain cascades and fountains and be at peace."*

56

Taking courage, Will decided to call home and see if he could have more time off. His folks willingly granted the extension, but wondered why he needed it. They asked no questions, however, and he kept the Lord's secret a while longer. He had found that God's work in a situation with an individual or a group of individuals is like a precious seed. It needs protection and nourishment in order to take form and grow. Will also wanted to be sure he was right in all this, that it was not just a wild goose chase. After all, there had been so many directions given them, the whole thing might exist only in their imaginations, although he seriously doubted this. Anyway, he had to be certain.

With the assurance of extra time, they proceeded east through New Carlisle to the little town of Paspebiac, where they stopped and talked to some highway workers eating lunch by the side of the road. Did any of them know of a farm for sale like the one they described? No, no one did. One suggested they stop at the Provincial Agricultural Station "up the road a piece" and inquire, and they did. The man there was very kind and, although a native Gaspesian, spoke good English and showed them one farm for sale. It was on a grassy mound, overlooking the sea. A dilapidated house sat on the property and there was also a barn that was close to caving in.

The three considered the house as a place they might buy (since it was low in price) to move their things into for winter storage, so they could search again the next spring. But as they prayed about that, it did not seem right. The Lord had told them to locate the property before winter and to prepare to move into it the following spring. Thanking their new friend, they moved on, with the promise of keeping in touch.

The road continued through Hopetown, St. Godfroi, and Shigawake. At Port Daniel they again came to a halt. Will was intuitively feeling that they were going too far east, and so was Marjorie. Linda was distressed and went into a little store to purchase sandwich materials. The children eagerly climbed out of the car, and the dog leaped after them.

They were close to the water in a charming salt-water bay with a beautiful beach. They could see little brooks running into the sea, and many species of birds. They were told that the rare black-crowned night heron nested there. Small picturesque houses crowded the cliffs and were spotted along the valley road that led inland to beautiful Port Daniel Park. They inquired about farms for sale and received no particular leads, but were told about the park and its campsites.

"Let's go there!" Betsy chirped from behind an ice-cream cone.

"I think that is a good idea," replied Marjorie. Linda spoke to Will who was gassing up the car, and he thought it was a good idea too. It was almost supper time and he was getting hungry. Linda purchased supper supplies and they turned onto a long dirt road that led into the park.

Linda and the children at Port Daniel Park

The friendly park manager showed them a pretty log cabin beside a mountain stream. It seemed just made for them. In the center of the cabin was a stove with a pile of wood waiting to be loaded in and lighted to warm them on that chilly evening. They all helped unload the car and prepare for the night while it was still light.

The scent of balsam fir hung heavy in the air. The smoke from other campers' fires drifted their way, bringing odors of frying bacon, steak, hash-browns, onions, and what-have-you. Oh, it was good to put their feet down for awhile. They settled in happily and released themselves to let the Lord do with them whatever He desired!

After supper the Bible was brought out and read aloud, prayers were offered in gratitude for a safe and pleasant day, meditation was entered, and the guidance of the Lord received. They were to reserve their cabin for another night, using Port Daniel Park as their base!

The morning again dawned bright and crisp. The searchers took time for devotions and then took walks into the woods and along the water's edge. By noon it was warm enough for the children to put on their swimsuits and play in the mountain brook that rippled over the rocks in front of the cabin. Linda wandered off alone, Will waded downstream, and Marjorie sat on a rock and contemplated the beauties of nature so lavishly spread around her. Interestingly enough, when they all convened that evening, each of them had picked up a small rock.

Linda had found a stone in the shape of a loaf of bread; it looked like an Easter loaf with the crisscrossed frosting on top. Will's rock was a circle with a dot in the center. Marjorie's small stone resembled the one upon which the Ten Commandments had been inscribed. There were even indentions that looked something like script.

Seeking the Lord's instruction the next morning, they learned they were to keep their camp for another night and continue the search. *"Seek your land today. Only true consecration to my worthy cause shall win. This means complete surrender unto me and my purposes for thy souls."* Jesus cautioned them to work together as a team. This was a new experience and they were enjoying it. Then, encouraging the children of the family, their Lord said, *"Thou hast done well, O little brother and sister. . . . Thou art chosen ones."*

On their journey this day, they were again led to backtrack southwest, systematically exploring all the narrow dirt roads that led off to the right into the hills of St. Jogues. At Bonaventure they explored the lonely colonies of St. Elzear and Thivierge; when they reached Caplan, they turned and went up to the colony of Ste. Claire. As usual, brick houses were rare. Probably bricks had to be imported and were more expensive than wood, which was available and cheap. Whatever the reason, there were very few brick houses. Perhaps the people did not like brick.

Weary from what appeared to be fruitless searching, they were cheered by the Lord's promise that they could return later that fall and continue the search *if need be.* There was much to see and learn. On their fourth day at the Park, they backtracked to Black Cape and up into the mountainous district of Querry and St. Edgar. The woods were heavily evergreen and there were no houses with a mountain east of them. They returned to the main road on the other side of the little Cascapedia River, passed Maria, and arrived at the tourist center of Carleton by the Sea, a lovely little village lying close to the seashore, where American bus tours stopped overnight and travelers searched for agates. Here in 1796, the first Post Office on the Gaspé Peninsula had been established. They went into a little museum of antique vehicles and learned that the town had received its name from Guy Carleton, who had participated in the capture of Quebec City under General Wolfe and later became Governor-General of British North America.

A sign on the long wharf offered fishing excursions for tourists. Space was also provided for freighters to load and unload lumber, fish, grain, and other items of trade. Carleton was a French-speaking village where commerce flourished. The fish co-op had apples from nearby orchards displayed for sale, as well as deep-sea fish.

The family stopped at the Agate Shop to see the local wares—beautiful agates gathered from the sea—but they did not loiter. There was more territory to explore on their last day before returning home. Several roads to the right led only to small districts of the same town. There was even a road that wound up Mont-St. Joseph to Notre Dame Oratory. At the top there stood a transmitting antenna, broadcasting French-language programs.

The view was extraordinary from the two thousand-foot summit—a beautiful panorama of beach and azure sea with little cottages and farms nestled amongst the hills. They met other Americans traveling on late fall vacations and exchanged notes. In the distance, they could trace the roadway by which they had come. The mountain road ended at the Oratory, so after offering a brief prayer and taking a second look at the magnificent view, they drove back down the mountain to the main highway, Route 6, turned right, and followed it to St. Omer.

Here they turned off again and traced a dirt road through Mission St. Louis to St. Louis de Gonzague. Although they were in high country, it did not resemble anything the Lord had shown them. Marjorie fidgeted and remarked that she wished they could explore the territory just beyond St. Omer and Drapeau. Farther on, the countryside did begin to look more like the area she had been shown, though the exact place was not to be seen.

Linda became intensely interested, too, as the land seemed to appear more similar to that she had seen. But it was again getting late, so the little group returned to Port Daniel Park to pack the car and prepare to leave for home very early the next morning. Will was restless and felt pressed to get back to work.

The family ate supper around the wood stove in their cozy cabin by the stream, trying to imbibe all the rich impressions they had received. As the last trace of sunshine streamed through the leafy boughs and the flowing water murmured contentedly, they settled in serenely for the night.

Before returning to their own country, they were encouraged by the Lord's words. *"Rejoice in your unison of purpose!"* Indeed, they were now of one mind, one heart, and one will, and that was to do the will of the Father. Had not their Savior said, I SEEK NOT MINE OWN WILL, BUT THE WILL OF THE FATHER WHICH HATH SENT ME (John 5:30b)? Nothing else would satisfy any of them now.

The Lord went on to say, *"Compare this trip to none, for thou hast been chosen for a unique purpose. . . . Do not cease thy search, for in seeking ye shall find! . . . Do not despair, but keep to thy high purpose!"* These words were confirmed by Philippians 3:14: I PRESS TOWARD THE MARK FOR THE PRIZE OF THE HIGH CALLING OF GOD IN CHRIST JESUS.

CHAPTER TEN

Where Is It?

Their last morning dawned bright and beautiful. Words from the Lord fell on tired ears. *"As ye return this day, behold! Let the Holy Spirit lead you off the highway occasionally. As thou sowest, so thou reapest. The farmer sows his farm with good seed and it springeth up into a good harvest! . . . Keep open to see thy valley as thou goest, for truly my spirit leadeth thee to a high, fertile valley—open and beautiful to behold. Fear not, O little flock, if thou findest not thy valley and mountain, but persevere in thy vision. . . . That which is mine shall come to thee later!"*

"Close thy quarters here and begin thy journey homeward. Travel at peace and rejoice for the day. Always be glad, even in trouble, and thus it dissolves."

How often God works His miracles at the eleventh hour! It takes training for those who would serve to remain alert at the last hour and not slumber in heedlessness. They remembered their Lord's words to His fatigued disciples on His last night in Gethsemane— COULDEST NOT THOU WATCH ONE HOUR? (Mark 14:37b).

The family said good-bye to the kind park director and to the campers around them. They gave their surplus food to their neighbors and left a few fresh tomatoes at the park director's door, then drove sadly down the long driveway and out onto the open road. "Good-bye, Port Daniel," the children called as they waved.

Route 6 had now become familiar territory, having traversed it four days in a row. Quickly they passed through the area that had taken them hours to investigate during the past days. Passing Carleton by the Sea and Drapeau, they entered the rustic French

63

town of Nouvelle. They did not know much about this little town of about three thousand, whose houses dotted the main highway. A limestone quarry on the right caught their attention, and Will swung off onto another narrow dirt road. After all, it might lead to their valley. They would not know unless they looked! But it dwindled off onto a cliff, where they had difficulty turning around to retrace their path. Farther on they rounded a corner, and there on the right was a river and, beside it, a road leading up into the mountains.

Will was excited. There was a river, there was a valley and a mountain, and there was a road leading up to it.

"Let's follow it!" he exclaimed.

But Linda was not at all convinced. "We are not supposed to be able to *see* the river," she reminded him. "But all right, let's go anyway and see what it's like up there."

This little dirt road was as narrow as many others had been. After half a mile it became an even narrower trail. They seemed to be slowly climbing up the side of a mountain and around it. To their left, through the dense foliage, they could dimly see the valley below them. At last there was a small wood road in which to turn around. As they came to a stop, Marjorie suddenly became excited. "Look at the foliage!" she exclaimed. "For the first time it is like the vegetation the Lord showed me in the vision, a combination of evergreens and hardwood trees!" Indeed, it was beautiful woodland.

Linda suggested that Will and Marjorie get out and look around. Marjorie, with compass in hand as usual, climbed out of the back seat, and Will enthusiastically jumped out of the front. Together they walked down a path until they emerged from the woods into a large sloping field filled with beautiful grain, rippling in the breeze. A barn stood in the middle of the field, but if there had been a house, it had long since vanished. They looked at the mountain behind them and down the hill at the scene before them.

The valley was long and flat, lovingly cradled between the mountains that rose on three sides. A river wound at the base of the mountain on the left and lazily found its way down to the sea at the valley's end. A low chain of mountains concealed the valley's northern boundary. Winding country roads led off into the distance. Farms and chalets dotted the landscape in a peaceful panorama.

Will took a deep breath. "Well!" he exclaimed, "This may not be our place, but if I had to live the rest of my life in a valley, this is the one I would choose. It's the most beautiful valley I have ever seen!"

"Yes, it certainly is!" Marjorie agreed wistfully. They both felt like explorers discovering a Tibetan Shangri-la for the first time. They stood transfixed over the beautiful scene.

Awaking to the passage of time they reluctantly returned to the car and reported to Linda that it was evidently not their valley. Bumping their way over the rough road back onto Route 6, they crossed a bridge and drove through a little settlement with a brick Post Office on their left and a road leading off to the right, down into the beautiful valley they had just seen from above.

"Let's take this road!" Will said excitedly. "I have a good feeling about it!"

The Valley Beautiful

65

"Oh, Will!" Marjorie kidded him. "That road is probably the same one we already followed on the other side of the valley. We have already seen it!"

"Don't bother," Linda added wearily. "The Post Office was supposed to be on the *right*, not the left."

"O.K.," Will replied resignedly. "Let's go home."

With that they ceased the search and drove the remaining five hundred miles west and south at full speed, none of them realizing that Linda had inadvertently *reversed* the vision the Lord had given her. She thought He was showing the Post Office to her from a western approach rather than from an eastern! This *was* their valley, but they drove on, leaving it behind!

Even while people are receiving extra help from the Lord, they are still prone to human mistakes. How carefully one needs to discern *all* the details of the Lord's prompting. Had He not said that very morning, *"Keep open to see thy valley as thou goest"*?

It was late when they finally arrived home tired and frustrated. Their search had taken them 2,400 miles (by the speedometer) over hard and difficult terrain; they had gone sometimes without sleep and food, had tramped endless miles—pressing on in answer to the Lord's call—but they had not located their Lord's place.

Will went to work the next day, Monday, but said little about his "vacation." The other greenhouse workers noticed he appeared a bit tired, but they only kidded him about his dirty new car.

During the following days the threesome rested whenever they had an opportunity. In a way they felt they had failed, yet deep in their hearts they wanted to believe that God's high and holy purpose was working out through them. They were like the man who pleaded with his Lord, I BELIEVE; HELP THOU MINE UNBELIEF (Mark 9:24). This may be the position of all humanity at times when the intellect argues against the Spirit.

Later, when they analyzed the leadings the Lord had given them, they wondered how they could have missed them. For example, when He had told them they would see their valley on the morning of their return home, they had believed, but only with *reservations*.

Now the threesome sought diligently for verification—to make sure each was intuitively connected with their Lord and Savior,

Jesus Christ, for He alone was their one desire. He assured them they were indeed very close to Him in thought, word, and intention, that their guidance was correct and they must *trust it*! They were to consider the trip they had just taken as a "stepping stone." From it they had learned patience, perseverance, tolerance, kindness, and courage. Their mutual understanding had broadened, though it needed more growth, and they had gained wisdom and faith as their souls were being knit together in an unshakable loyalty and love of God.

But Sparkie had decided he would have no more of the matter. Perhaps his family would go, but he would stay behind. Although advanced in years, he had been very healthy until and during the trip. But suddenly he became ill—very ill—and even after much prayer there was no improvement. When Will and Linda took him to the veterinarian, the horrible pronouncement of cancer was made.

Sparkie became weaker and weaker each day. The illness appeared to advance quickly, and within a short time he was so feeble he was placed on the living room couch on a blanket, fed with a spoon, and carried bodily outside to go to the bathroom. Sparkie was greatly loved by one and all, especially by Will. This was a real shock to him, almost like an insurmountable wall, since he also at this time was struggling with emotional ties to his parents and the home place where he had always lived and worked.

One day as Sparkie was close to his last breath, a relative visited, and the adults, with the two children, knelt beside their pet. Laying hands on him and humbly asking the Lord, Jesus Christ, to heal him, they prayed. Immediately Sparkie lifted his head and seemed to be smiling at the little group. Soon he moved and got up off the couch, apparently feeling better. Shortly afterward, he walked around the room. He appeared hungry and drank the milk offered him.

From that time on, he became stronger and stronger. He had been completely healed! Praise God! This, on October 5, was only the first of many healings as a result of their prayers. THE LORD IS GREAT, AND GREATLY TO BE PRAISED! (Ps. 96:4).

God was already victorious; had not Jesus Christ won the crown?

BE OF GOOD CHEER; I HAVE OVERCOME THE WORLD, He said (John 16:33 c)—and that meant every evil thing in the world! What was cancer to the Lord of Hosts?

They learned that most of the ills of humankind come from disobedience to the Holy Spirit, which operates through the conscience. As they learned to obey the inner guidance more carefully, they were able to be of more service to those around them.

Interestingly enough, casual friends began stopping in at random. They asked questions about God and how He works in their lives. Will and Linda became willing channels of loving help to people they hardly knew, those who were reaching out to God and blindly groping for a higher understanding of spiritual things. Marjorie found her ministry increasing as she obediently responded to the Lord, putting God first. *"Bend to my wishes instead of thine own,"* He cautioned her.

One morning shortly after their return, they were told to prepare for the move ahead by cleaning their closets and selling things they no longer had use for. They were to retain the essentials needed in their new work and housekeeping and dispose of the rest. They were even to begin buying certain items that took time to order—items that would be needed in their new operation in Canada next spring.

The Lord assured them their land was safe and advised them not to delay their plans for their move. *"Great joy lies in the work and its reward, when it is accomplished in the spirit of love, faithfulness, and forgiveness. . . . Behold, I prepare a place north of this and east. Come and taste, for its land is sweet and its honeycomb flavorful, its hills are vaulted and domed in the heavens, its valley lieth green and fertile."*

Visions came frequently for Linda and Marjorie now, but Will sat morning after morning, gaining biblical insight, but without visionary specifics of the farm.

"How come I can't get a vision of the farm, too?" he inquired. "It seems this place is just as much mine as yours, and the Lord should show *me* some of the details, as well as showing them to you two!" He was growing exasperated.

"Just be patient," Marjorie advised. . . . "Ask Jesus Christ to show you something of importance regarding the place, and He surely will. The Lord is faithful to those who trust in Him!"

"O.K., Lord," Will asked, "please show me something this morning You want me to know about the farm in Canada." They all remained quiet and meditated on the words they had just read from their Bible. The half-hour meditation passed quickly and soon it was time to begin their workday. As Linda picked up the Bible and they all stood to go their various ways, Marjorie looked at Will. He seemed strangely quiet and passive.

"Did you receive anything?" she asked.

"No, not really," he replied. "It couldn't have been a vision from the Lord. It must have been my own imagination . . . although I have never really seen one exactly like that before."

Both Linda and Marjorie came to attention. Sitting down again, they asked in unison, "What was it? Did you see something, Will? Tell us!"

"Well," he began hesitantly, "it seems I saw sort of a garage structure—I entered a building, and to my left I saw the right rear wheel of a tractor. It was a big yellow wheel with a new tire. I walked ahead on the right side of the tractor, and I saw that the main body of the machine was red and had some yellow writing on it. It looked hand-lettered but I couldn't read it. Next I saw the small front wheel, which was also yellow, with an old car tire on it. I walked around to the front and saw that the grillwork was painted alternately red and yellow. There was an exhaust pipe painted silver that came out the top, and an unusual lever stuck out the back, but I didn't know what its purpose was. The colors were very vivid. But it probably wasn't a vision from the Lord," he added. "You know how I have loved tractors all my life."

They all agreed that probably the Lord would never consider a tractor important enough for a vision. But they noted Will's report for future reference, if need be.

CHAPTER ELEVEN

Alone, but Not Alone

How they yearned to locate their new home! Two weeks had elapsed when Marjorie asked the Lord if she should go alone to look for it. Receiving His go-ahead, they got the big map out and carefully inspected it. A shallow part of the Appalachian mountain range crossed the province of New Brunswick. The tour guide had said that area was predominantly English speaking; about one-third of the population was French, and there were some Indians.

Marjorie was especially interested in the mountainous areas, since the Lord had told them their Canadian farm was in a high, fertile valley. Since this province was similar to Quebec, possibly there might be mountain foliage similar to the kind they had found in the Carleton and Nouvelle area, which tallied with the visions the Lord had given them. Also, there should be valleys bordered by rivers—even the brick house might be there!

Leaving the possibility of Quebec temporarily behind, Marjorie scanned the map more closely. The town closest to the high peaks appeared to be Plaster Rock, not far from Mt. Carleton, 2,690 feet high.

"Maybe I should go and see what it's like," Marjorie questioned.

"You might find a bear that you can *love*," Will replied, with a twinkle in his eye.

"Oh, Will," Linda interjected, "will you ever forget the black-fly incident?"

"Never!" Will replied grimly. Smiling broadly, he added, "Of course, they couldn't resist—I'm so sweet!"

It was finally decided that Marjorie would set out on Friday,

October 6, leaving Linda in charge of her group of parishioners for the Sunday service.

Giving Marjorie a parting prayer of protection, Will and Linda and the two children stood waving goodbye as her white convertible turned onto the highway. Her first stop was to be Portland, Maine, where she would minister to friends that weekend.

Marjorie awoke Monday to a beautiful day. As she drove, a cloud of radiant light appeared in the sky ahead of her car. She felt the fresh anointing of the Lord's presence and sang praises and hymns as she proceeded north and east.

As the day wore on, she decided to rest for a while by the wayside, read her Bible, and pray. Drawing to the side on a deserted stretch of road, she opened the trunk of her car, got out her Bible, and tossed in her jacket. Slamming down the trunk lid, she got back in the car and read for a while. It was such an inspiration to read and pray, way out here in the country.

As three o'clock drew near, she decided to drive on and reached for her keys. Oh, no! She had put them in her jacket pocket and locked them in the trunk! There was no way to get the trunk open; there was even a steel divider between the trunk and the back seat.

"All right, God," Marjorie said peacefully. "I am Yours, and I just made a mistake. Please send along some help quickly. Thank You, Father." Then she continued reading until a policeman finally stopped. He called a tow truck, and the car was towed to the nearest garage, where they forced a small opening into the truck from the back seat, reached in, and fished the keys out of her jacket pocket.

On her way again, Marjorie could still see the radiant cloud in front of her. It remained visible until she reached her destination and served as an assurance that God was with her and all was well. She needed that assurance as she traveled into strange territory alone (but not alone!).

During that morning's devotions, the Lord had impressed her with the idea that many new experiences lay ahead. She might be tempted to become very discouraged, but she was not to give up. If she would release self-will completely, He would *lead* her directly to the place she sought—the place of His own choosing.

The idea of releasing self-will is very pleasant to contemplate, but not easy to exercise. Unfortunately, self-will is a very evasive thing, not easily recognizable. Marjorie prayed continually as she drove northward on Route 95 to Houlton, Maine. Here she turned, and crossed into Canada at Woodstock, heading north for the high ground of Plaster Rock. Would this be *the* right place? Only time would tell!

Her excitement increased as she neared Plaster Rock, but the closer she came, the less it bore any resemblance to the vision. The land was high, yes, but the timber had been cut, leaving large bald spots, naked rocks, and hillside farms with sparse grasslands. Driving over a dirt road laid out on top of a domed hill, she came to the town and stopped at an inn for the night. Men with high boots and beards came and went—foresters and miners—it was a man's country, where women were in the minority.

The next day she quickly explored the territory, trying desperately to do the Lord's bidding. Fortunately, He judges not by deed, but by heart's intent! It was more than obvious that this was not the land the Lord had promised them. By ten o'clock she was ready to leave. Turning her car east, Marjorie followed Route 109 for about fifty miles into dense, uninhabited woodland. She was reminded, HE SHALL GIVE HIS ANGELS CHARGE OVER THEE (Ps. 91:11). Seeing no trace of an open valley or a variegated forest, she turned around in a rutted wood road, returned to Plaster Rock, and followed Route 385 through the Blue Mountains to Oxbow and Everett, on to Riley Brook, and then to Nictau, where four rivers met and the road ended. There was but one road in and out. Lovely hemlock and balsam boughs swept the car at places, crystal mountain streams ran beside the road, and overhead the sun now shone brightly.

Time was passing. In examining her map, checking for places she had not seen before, Marjorie noticed that a large portion of country extended north toward the St. Lawrence River in Quebec. Rimouski Park, with its three mountains, was in that section, along with many lakes and promising valleys.

Turning the once white car around, she headed north on Route 2 toward Grand Falls and Edmundston, New Brunswick. Crossing the border at Ste. Rose-du-Degele into Quebec, she drove inland. There the terrain was rough and, for the most part, sparsely settled.

She drove up and down hills, through virgin forests, and beside rushing streams filled with rainbow trout. At places the road was precarious, with no guardrails for protection against the sheer dropoffs into deep chasms below. Surely God's angels were with her throughout that trip into the rugged, undeveloped country. St. Michel-du-Squatec afforded lodging for the night.

The next morning during devotions, she was impressed with the feeling that she was going in the *right* direction and that she should continue eastward. Moving quickly on, she continued her search. With the added visions of Linda's Main Street, brick Post Office, valley road and river, and Will's red and yellow tractor, there were now twenty-eight prerequisites that must be met.

Moose, porcupine, deer, and other wild life, appeared beside the road, as Marjorie traveled over terrain quite unlike any she had seen before. One road continued on—and on—and on—and on—until it finally reached an intersection. There she went into a little general store to ask the way. She inquired politely in her best French, but even her best was unintelligible to the dear folk trying to help her. She could not even find out where she was!

After many more miles of wilderness driving, the road ended at a beautiful lake. An empty house stood on the shore, lonely and forsaken. Turning around, she had to travel the whole, long, dusty road to get back to the same intersection!

The new territory through which she began to pass resembled an accordian—or better still, a roller coaster! The road went straight up to the top of each rise and then straight down on the other side so sharply Marjorie was frightened lest her car catapult. She reminded herself that THE LORD SHALL PRESERVE THEE FROM ALL EVIL (Ps. 121:7). Mile after mile of the roller-coaster road unfolded. The hills became so steep, and the drop over the top so sudden, there was no way to know whether another car might be approaching from the other direction. This was a time of prayer for protection, and Marjorie prayed continuously. At last this road also ended, but there was no other, to right or left. Once again she was left to retrace the distance she had just covered. This could easily have been a terrifying experience, had she not kept her eyes on the bright cloud ahead and had faith in God's ever-loving care and protection.

Marjorie continued her journey eastward toward Highway 6, which cut across the western neck of the Gaspé Peninsula. Here, too, was undeveloped country, with lakes, summer campgrounds, and occasional small villages with brightly painted houses, clustered close together as a fortress against the wilderness that rapped continually at their doors. Exploring each nook and cranny that came into view, she noticed that night was fast approaching.

She began to feel frustrated and discouraged. Should she return home without finding the farm? She had looked and looked, to no avail! Her car was brown with dust, but not a trace of the place could she find. Perhaps she should go to the park at Port Daniel? Or better still, perhaps she should now examine the Matapedia area and look behind the mountains of Carleton, Nouvelle, and Escuminac, where the foliage had appeared to resemble that in their visions.

Many thoughts came to her that night in the motel at Pointe-a-la-Croix. This town was on the Quebec side of a fairly new bridge that connected Quebec with New Brunswick. The former ferryboat landing still remained intact below the bridge.

When Marjorie asked the Lord's assistance the next morning, she was told to go ahead and see the special land before her—for "*it was surely there*"! What more did she need? She still needed to release the idea that *she* would find the place. She had forgotten that the Lord had said *he would lead her there!* There is nothing wrong with serving the Lord, and there is nothing wrong with trying one's level best, but when God has spoken, He has spoken!

That day Marjorie drove to the little village of Maria and up into the mountains. The foliage looked familiar, but there was no brick house, nor was the valley correct according to the visions the Lord had given her. No—nothing was quite right.

CHAPTER TWELVE

Friends in the North

As night drew near, Marjorie found herself in the area of Nouvelle. There were no motels, and it seemed too far to go back to Pointe-a-la-Croix. A little sign hung invitingly on a neat white house by the side of the road caught her attention—a guest house! She drove in. A pretty French woman welcomed her.

"I have just one guest room, and you may have it," she exclaimed hospitably in good English. It seems the woman's sister and her husband owned the place, but they were away on vacation. She and her husband were tending the guest house in their absence. She explained how nice it was for them to stay there, since their house was being built but was not yet finished.

This beautiful French woman and her husband were soon to play an important part in God's plan. Interestingly, her sister had wanted to take down the sign before leaving but had not done so. Had the sign not been up, Marjorie would not have stopped. The next morning she bade her new friends good-bye and continued the search. Driving west toward the neck of the peninsula, she passed through Restigouche and came to the little village of Matapedia, wedged between the mountains and the river, with its rushing waterfalls. A railroad bridge, a freight car on a sidetrack, a cluster of houses and shops close to the edge of the deep-banked, swiftly flowing river—all fitted themselves into the tiny space left beside an old Indian trail, now a state highway, Route 6.

Here some English was spoken and a shopkeeper told her the river was famous for its 222 rapids and its salmon fishing. The thought of a home-baked salmon dinner swirled in her mind, but she pressed on.

To her right, signs pointed to various hamlets. Following the first, she drove up what appeared to be the side of a steep cliff. Following the leveled roadway she eventually came to a settlement in a bare and lonely spot.

Returning, she resolved to follow the next, labeled St. Fidele. She obviously was not taking the tourist route! Again the road led straight up—to heaven? No, not quite that far! It leveled off and continued through dense woodland, past mountain streams, and into another colony. It was interesting to observe how Canada had endeavored to locate colonies so carefully for its early new immigrants. Again, the hamlet was on a hilltop, with no hint of a fertile valley or any of the landmarks she sought.

Retracing her route, she wondered how the inhabitants ever managed to get down such a steep road in wintertime. She thought of the old fairy tale of the princess on the glass hill. She later learned that people in that region wore what they called grippers—metal claws fastened to the soles of their boots; these enabled them to walk safely during the ice season, which sometimes lasted for months.

Retracing the path again, Marjorie became engrossed in following dirt trails into the mountains, where she saw a few waterfalls and also noticed the presence of cedar trees, which the Lord had prophesied would be on their property in abundance. However, nothing else looked "right."

An insignificant dirt road in Escuminac ended at last in a beautiful valley. To her left, a white house sat beside a barn and a quiet river flowed between the house and the roadway. The valley stretched off between the mountains in pastoral loveliness, as cows grazed contentedly. To her right rose a sheer and densely wooded mountain.

Crossing the tiny handmade bridge, Marjorie met the English farmer, who came out of his house to greet her. He was not the man she had seen in her vision, nor was the house brick, but she was intensely interested. Could this possibly be the valley? She asked if there were also a brick house? No, He knew of no brick house—in fact, this house was *the* house—and Marjorie's compass showed that the mountain was not east.

This was a time of inner questioning. Maybe she had not received the visions correctly. Maybe it wasn't a brick house, she should look for, after all. Maybe—maybe—maybe . . . many doubts assailed her as she stood there silently gazing across the valley to the mountains, whose foliage was quite similar to that which the Lord had shown her.

"Do you mind if I take a little walk just to look around?" she inquired.

"No, of course not," the man replied kindly. Walking off, she found a pretty spot where she could sit down and pray. As she talked with the Lord, she put to Him all the questions that had assailed her and ended by asking, was this their valley?

She could actually feel the Lord smiling over the whole matter. Treating her deep concern lightly, He suggested she ask the farmer if he wanted to sell his property. The Lord said, *"Listen carefully, for I speak through others."*

Returning to the farmer, Marjorie thanked him for allowing her to walk around. Then she asked if he would consider selling the place, and she listened carefully for his answer.

"What, me sell this place? Not on your life! I was born here and I intend to die here—and after that my son will have the place. Never will it be sold!!!"

Well, that ended that. How could she doubt what the Lord was telling her? Thanking the farmer, she got into her car, waved good-bye, and drove off.

Now it was getting late and she must find a place for the night. Looking at her map, Marjorie found she was only one town removed from Nouvelle and the nice guest house. Why not go back there? It seemed logical, although she felt a little embarrassed, since she had said good-bye to them just that morning. However, she drove back, and the couple greeted her warmly. Madame S asked if she wanted the same room. Yes, she would be grateful, Marjorie replied. There were a few more places she wanted to explore the next day.

She rose early, enjoyed her usual Bible reading, prayers, and meditations, and again said good-bye to the friendly couple. Most of the day was uneventful. More dust, more narrow, winding roads, more wilderness—although the area was beautiful she was feeling discouraged and very tired. She had gone so far and found so little that measured up!

That morning the Lord had told her to bring to mind the visions He had given her, remembering them accurately in every detail. She realized she had almost forgotten the details and had to work diligently to bring them back. She asked the Lord to help her. This He did as she sat quietly in her car by the roadside, looking down from the heights to the highway that wound along below by the peaceful sea.

Retracing Route 6 to the point where she had stopped exploring the day before, she passed the same road the threesome had taken on their first journey—the mountain road that had led to a view of the beautiful valley.

Continuing along the main highway, she drove across a bridge, came to a brick Post Office, and noticed a road leading northward into the valley—the *same* road Will had wanted to take on the way home, when she and Linda had discouraged him. She was sure it connected with the dirt road on the other side of the valley, but she took it anyway, just to be certain.

The valley road passed a couple of peaceful farms with cows grazing in the fields and, after a short distance, divided. One fork passed over a bridge to the right; the other continued straight on, farther into the valley. Marjorie took the latter, which wound along by the river bank and soon ended in a barnyard. Had she continued, she would have driven straight into a barn, where she might have found a cow in need of milking, or any number of farm duties! Not especially desiring to spend her day in a barn, she backed carefully between a couple of apple trees and retreated before the farmer decided to put her to work.

"Well, thank You, Father!" Marjorie remarked out loud. Driving out of sight of the farm, she parked by the side of the road and sought biblical support. Opening the Book at random, she read, AND, BEHOLD, I AM WITH THEE, AND WILL KEEP THEE IN ALL PLACES WHITHER THOU GOEST, AND WILL BRING THEE AGAIN INTO THIS LAND; FOR I WILL NOT LEAVE THEE, UNTIL I HAVE DONE THAT WHICH I HAVE

SPOKEN TO THEE OF (Genesis 28:15). This supported the beautiful promises the Lord had given, if the threesome would go and do as He asked.

The river boundary that wasn't noticed

Returning to the bridge, Marjorie noticed that the river ran along beside the road by which she had come. It had not been visible because it had worn its course deeply into the hollow of the land and was bordered by bushes that made the woodland appear to be continuous. With this observation, the flame of hope flickered.

Looking up the river, hoping to spot a brick house, she saw instead two pretty chalets silhouetted by mountain beauty. What a lovely valley this is, she thought. Driving on, she came to an intersection. She decided not to take the road leading right, since she was sure it must connect with the same road they had followed previously on the other side of the valley.

Turning left, she followed the other side of the stream up to a logging camp in the tall timber. Here the rutted single lane ended and nothing but a wood road, passable only by jeep, led farther. She returned to the intersection and turned into a fascinating dirt road that also led up into the mountains, its narrow S curves at times dropping steeply into gorges where waterfalls spilled their silvery streams.

Coming suddenly out of the dense forest, Marjorie found herself on a large, open plateau, where roads led off in all directions, seemingly to nowhere. Gaining a high vantage point, she gazed into the distance to see if any towns were visible—but she was surrounded by nothing but a vast wilderness. This was another abandoned colony. People had been moved in, cut down the forest for firewood, and had been moved out again by the Canadian government. Choosing a road, she continued on it until it became impassable. Backing down the rocky hillside, she managed to turn around in a narrow wood road, barely missing a drop into the ravine below.

Returning to the intersection in the valley was a real treat. The scenery was unusually lovely. Some of the hills arched gracefully, with pastures saddling them in soft strips of grey-green. Others were cone-shaped and wood roads wove interesting patterns through their timberlines. These were like David's LITTLE HILLS that SKIPPED . . . LIKE LAMBS (Ps. 114:4b). Rushing streams followed the road and ran out into inviting meadows and open fields, where sun-ripened wheat awaited harvesting.

Since she would probably never see this place again, Marjorie took pictures as a remembrance of the valley beautiful. Then with a last prayer she went on, past the road she had not taken because she was so sure where it went, and again found herself on "Main Street," Route 6, wondering where she would spend the night. She really didn't want to return to the same guest house, after saying good-bye twice before. But there was no other place to stay! She felt pushed (by the Lord) to return there, embarrassed or not.

She rang the front doorbell, and was greeted by the same lovely woman, who reached out and gathered her into a warm, friendly embrace.

"Come in, come in—we really didn't expect to see you *again!*"

"No—well, I—that is—I needed a place to stay for the night and thought of you. . . . Do you still have the room available, or is someone else using it?"

"Yes, yes! It is empty—just waiting for you!" she declared with enthusiasm. "Come, I will show you!"

She took Marjorie up the stairs and threw open the door. Sure enough, it was just as Marjorie had left it, except the bed had been freshly made and the room aired. Marjorie didn't know at the time, but in Madame S's eyes, she resembled a beloved sister who had recently died. Perhaps this was the reason for the extra warm welcome!

Moving a bit closer, Madame softly inquired, "This is your third visit here, yes?"

"Yes," Marjorie replied.

Madame S's eyebrows puckered and she paused. "Why are you still here? I thought you were going home to the States?" she asked.

"Well, I *was* going home," Marjorie tried to explain, "but I was delayed a bit."

"Oh, I see. Are you looking for someone or something?"

Marjorie hesitated. She had told very few people about her real mission here. Should she tell this woman, or not? Responding to the warmth that reached out to her weary soul, Marjorie confessed simply, "Well, to tell the truth, I'm looking to buy a farm."

"A farm?" Eyebrows again went up. "Well, I, eh, don't know. I'll tell you, though. Why don't you have breakfast with my husband and me tomorrow morning, and we can talk about it. All right?"

"Oh, I couldn't eat here," Marjorie replied, "unless you let me pay you for my breakfast as though I were at a restaurant. I wouldn't want to impose on your kindness."

"That doesn't matter a bit!" the woman replied emphatically. "You plan to eat with us in the morning! O.K.?" And so it was settled.

This was a much needed note of kindness. Marjorie felt she had failed. She had to admit that all her searching had come to naught. She had been unable to locate the property the Lord had promised them. She would return home in the morning.

"May I use your phone to make a long distance collect call?" Marjorie asked as the lady descended the stairs.

"Of course you can. Just use the extension in your room!" was the reply. "Have a good sleep!"

Marjorie called home. When Linda and Will were on the other end of the line, "I give up," she confided. "I just can't find the place. I've looked everywhere! I'm starting home tomorrow morning."

"Don't give up!" Linda pleaded. "Release personal responsibility. The Lord has done it! Let it happen!"

Will added, "God is with you, and we are too, in Spirit, anyway."

"We are praying with you, Mom," Linda added. "Have you released your *personal* responsibility?"

"I believe so," Marjorie replied. "At least I have *tried* to."

"Well, let's have a prayer now over the phone to help you release it *all* to Him, shall we?" Linda suggested.

"Yes," agreed Will. "Let your cares go and give them to the Lord!"

They took heart as they prayed out loud in turn.

"We will pray diligently with you tonight," said Will. "Release it to God and have a good rest."

"Yes! Let Him *do the leading,* Mom!" Linda advised again. "We love you!"

"Yes," Will agreed. "Whether you find the place or not, we love you!"

What more could Marjorie desire? she had the love of God, the love of her daughter and son-in-law, the friendship of the guest-house couple—God had showered her with love and tender care throughout the entire trip. A well of deep gratitude sprang up in her and, with a shaky voice, Marjorie thanked them, assured them of her love, and hung up.

"Father," she prayed tearfully, "forgive my shortsightedness. I see but a fraction of your great whole, I know."

She took out her Bible, opened to First Timothy, and read, FIGHT THE GOOD FIGHT OF FAITH, LAY HOLD ON ETER-

NAL LIFE, WHEREUNTO THOU ART ALSO CALLED, AND HAST PROFESSED A GOOD PROFESSION BEFORE MANY WITNESSES (6:12).

Turning to Philippians, she read, I PRESS TOWARD THE MARK FOR THE PRIZE OF THE HIGH CALLING OF GOD IN CHRIST JESUS. . . . AND THE PEACE OF GOD, WHICH PASSETH ALL UNDERSTANDING, SHALL KEEP YOUR HEARTS AND MINDS THROUGH CHRIST JESUS (3:14, 4:7).

Her thoughts turned to Paul and his struggles on the roadway of life. Probably there were many times of weariness and despair when he was trying to find certain people or houses. Yet he never gave up hope—nor would she! Then and there, she relinquished her personal ideas of how to find the farm. She released the search to Him. It was now entirely in the Lord's hands. A deep peace filled her soul and she fell asleep.

That evening after the phone call, Linda felt very sad about her mother's trials in finding the land. Both Will and Linda were very discouraged and felt great pity for Marjorie.

The Bible says, THOU TELLEST MY WANDERINGS: PUT THOU MY TEARS INTO THY BOTTLE: ARE THEY NOT IN THY BOOK? WHEN I CRY UNTO THEE, THEN SHALL MINE ENEMIES TURN BACK: THIS I KNOW; FOR GOD IS FOR ME. IN GOD WILL I PRAISE HIS WORD: . . . IN GOD HAVE I PUT MY TRUST (Ps. 56:8-10 a, 11a).

After prayer and Bible reading, Will and Linda used the usual statement for insulation before meditation: "I am surrounded by the great white light of God. Nothing but good do I give out, nothing but good do I receive." As she said this, Linda had a vision of an angel, beautiful to behold, with golden hair bound in braids around her head. The winged visitor neither spoke nor moved, but indicated intense mercy and love toward Linda, suggesting great sympathy and aid for their cause.

There were many times when the threesome was aware of divine intervention in their behalf, and they suspect that this occurs for many people, more often than they realize. In this case, the angelic assistant was visually seen.

CHAPTER THIRTEEN

God Doesn't Lie!

Another morning, beautiful and clear, dawned in Nouvelle. Marjorie dressed quickly, packed and had devotions, then went downstairs quietly so as not to awaken the good folks in the guest house. She had decided to have breakfast somewhere on the way home. She was through looking! She had resigned her job, had turned it totally over to the Lord.

As she sneaked down the last few steps and turned the corner into the kitchen, she was greeted with the fragrance of coffee and a friendly "Hello!" Both Madame S and her husband were seated at a cheery breakfast table, set for three.

"Come, sit down and join us," said Madame S as she got up and pulled out a chair for her guest. "How are you this morning?"

"I'm just fine," Marjorie replied emphatically. She had not felt so free since the trip began. What a joy it was to release all cares to the Lord! She evidently had been overly concerned for a longer period than she had realized. She wanted to jump up from the table and shout for joy in the Lord, but she didn't. Instead, "How are *you*?"

"Oh, all right, I guess," was the reply. "I could hardly sleep all night. I kept praying and praying and asking God, What shall I do? Shall I tell her, or shan't I tell her? Oh my, I had a tiring night!"

"Really?" Marjorie was startled.

"Oh yes, it's true! You see, Mrs. Russell, my brother has a farm for sale. No sign up, you understand. But it's for sale."

The wheels began turning in Marjorie's head. Probably just another farm in the hills somewhere. I'll not become excited over this one! "Oh?" she replied.

"Yes!" Madame S said, nodding her head and waving her hand in a westerly direction. "It's over there. It's a nice brick house! Would you like to see it?"

"Brick house?" Marjorie repeated dumbly. Again she thought, I won't get excited, because it is probably not *the* brick house, and I'm not going to buy the wrong place.

"Yes, it's a brick house, very nice. Maybe you will like it. It has a barn and lots of land. Shall I call him and see if he might show it to you today?"

"Well, I'm on my way home now, but if he wants to show it to me early this morning, that will be fine," Marjorie replied casually.

Madame S hastily telephoned, and yes, they would show Marjorie the farm that morning. Monsieur S kindly offered to guide her to it by going ahead of her in his car.

All the way, Marjorie kept praying, "Dear Lord, don't let me get my hopes up and then dash them again. Keep me calm and controlled. It would be just too much to hope that this could be the place . . . too many prerequisites to meet . . . just humanly impossible. . . . Oh, dear," she interrupted her thought, "where is my faith? I guess I must have left it somewhere on a mountain in the dusty blue distance. Lord, forgive me!"

Marjorie now felt very strange. She was following the other car down "Main Street," Route 6, when they arrived at the little brick Post Office on the left. Mr. S swung right onto the valley road— the road she had followed the day before, the *same road Will had wanted to take.*

She meekly followed, praising God for friends, even when they were strangers. The car ahead turned right, crossed over the bridge, and came to a halt at the intersection. Yes, Marjorie knew this place all right! She had followed the road to the left into a logging camp and the road straight ahead to the deserted colony and waterfall. But Monsieur S turned abruptly to the right.

Oh, she thought, this is the road that joins the one on the other side of the valley, the one I have already seen! They passed a corner grocery store and proceeded up the road. Suddenly a brick house came into view. It had been there all the time, and as she had passed by on the "colony" road, she could have looked over and seen it! (Had the Lord veiled it from her eyes? Hadn't He said *He* would lead her to it?)

Main house

Monsieur S swung into the yard, drove down the hill toward the barn, and parked. Marjorie followed him and stopped in front of the barn. Getting out of her car, she stood transfixed! She was looking up the hill at the house from the same angle the Lord had shown it to her in the vision . . . a brick house, two stories high, and a two-story extension. It was as though the invisible realm had suddenly spun a gossamer web, making her vision manifest. There before her was the reality of her Lord's prophecy, and He had chosen this kind, humble man as His guiding vessel.

King David's psalm of gratitude flooded in upon her: THE LORD

IS MY SHEPHERD; I SHALL NOT WANT. HE MAKETH ME TO LIE DOWN IN GREEN PASTURES: HE LEADETH ME BESIDE THE STILL WATERS. HE RESTORETH MY SOUL: HE LEADETH ME . . . (23:1-3a). *He leadeth me!* How true.

Drawing her thought back to her vision of the house, she asked, "But where is the front door?"

"The front door?" Monsieur S replied, "Why, that was taken out years ago and a bathroom put in the space. Look—see where the bricks are missing—that is where the front door *used* to be—I mean, when they thought the road was coming down this way near the barn—I mean, when the house was originally built—*before* they had a barn." Backing away a bit and scrutinizing her, he continued, "How did you know there was a front door there?"

The "special front" door (back of main house)

87

Before she could collect her breath, the back door opened and out stepped the same two people the Lord had shown her. They came toward her and welcomed her warmly. This was like walking and talking in a dream. The whole thing was so amazing Marjorie could hardly believe her eyes. But, yes, it was true!

The tall lean man and short robust woman asked her in to see the house. Marjorie walked behind them like a robot. Nodding and smiling, the woman pointed out the rooms and the special closets where she kept everything neat and tidy. She was an expert home-maker! Marjorie marveled at her superior orderliness. The varnished floor gleamed so brightly in the morning sun that they could have had breakfast on it, in perfect comfort.

Marjorie observed everything in a daze. The woman showed her the spinning wheel and the wool she was spinning. Yes, they had had lots of sheep on their farm at one time. Yes, they had raised flax and had made linen there, too. Yes, she did weave!

From room to room Marjorie followed, saying little as they spoke to her in English far better than her French. They were kind, gentle people, and she loved them, though she hardly knew them.

They went upstairs and finally reached the attic over the two-story extension.

"This is where I dry my clothes in bad weather," the owner's wife explained. Marjorie was so awestruck she could hardly think. She didn't even count the rooms. This was the right place!

Downstairs again, Marjorie got out her compass. There were the mountains rimming the valley—so beautiful and fertile. Looking straight out the front window she pointed her compass at the mountain she supposed was part of the farm . . . and her heart sank! The compass read NE!

"Oh," she said out loud with a disappointed gesture, "the mountain is northeast, not east!"

"Yes, yes," the farmer agreed, speaking rapidly in French as he waved his arm to the right. Monsieur S explained that that mountain was not their land. The farmland in the valley was laid out at an angle from the road. *Their* mountain was over to the right. Pointing her compass toward the mountain that was part of the farm, she read E! She could almost hear the Lord: *"This is East."*

"Oh, God, I believe—forgive my unbelief!" she murmured silently and gratefully.

"What do you raise on your farm?" she enquired.

"Oh, wheat, oats, rye, barley, buckwheat," the farmer replied.

"Yes, Lord," Marjorie said in her heart, "just as You told us!"

"And they had turkeys and chickens once—lots of them," Monsieur S added.

"Of course," Marjorie agreed.

"Would you like to see the river?" Monsieur S asked. "He is saying he will drive you down there. It bounds the property."

"Oh, yes! I would *love* to see the river!" Marjorie was exuberant. She and the farmer drove slowly behind the barn and over the fields to the river bank. Walking to the drop-off, she saw the river down below—wide, shallow, with rocks in the bottom, and invisible from the road—exactly as Linda had described it.

"Beautiful!" Marjorie breathed.

"Yes, yes! Very nice!" the farmer responded enthusiastically.

"You want to see the other side too—near the mountain?" he motioned. "I'll take you!"

Getting in the car, they drove back to the house, across the road, and toward the mountain that rose high above the fields. It was a lot farther across the valley than she had estimated. Distances here in Canada were vast! She loved the airiness and the crystal stream they forded. They passed cedars, and she remarked on them. (Another of the Lord's prerequisites!)

"Yes, plenty of them—all over the place," the farmer gestured and smiled. He was obviously amused at her astonishment over such commonplace things as brick houses, rivers, mountains to the east, and cedar trees!

When they finally arrived at the base of the mountain, Marjorie got out and began to climb up the steep slope.

"No, no!" the farmer cried in alarm. "Don't do that. No! Too steep!" Marjorie had wanted to see more of the forest, but he was right. The mountain rose sharply straight up, and there was little to cling to on the rocky crags. How trees managed to grow there was a miracle, she thought as she remembered her vision.

Driving back, Marjorie was still in a state of joyous bewilderment. With all the previous months of preparation, now that the prophecies were actually being fulfilled, she could scarcely take it all in!

Linda driving Will's miracle tractor

The biggest surprise of all came last. As they walked toward the house, the farmer said, "How would you like to see my garage? A tractor goes with the place!"

"Did you say a *tractor?*" Marjorie asked incredulously.

"Yes, yes, a tractor. You come and see!" He led the way.

Flinging open the garage door, he stood aside for her to enter. To her left Marjorie saw a tractor—first the large yellow rear wheel with a new tire, then the red body with the hand-lettered words *Massey Harris* in yellow, then the small front wheel with a worn car tire, and on the front, the grillwork alternating red and yellow. A silver smokestack was sticking up, and behind the driver's seat was a strange-looking lever.

"What is that?" Marjorie asked, pointing to it.

Oh, that?" the farmer laughed. "That is different. The old one broke. I make new myself!"

To see visions and to hear prophecies is one thing, but to actually watch them coming to pass in our three-dimensional realm is awe inspiring, to say the least. The visions were living miracles. The tractor vision had seemed foolish to the threesome, but certainly GOD HATH CHOSEN THE FOOLISH THINGS OF THE WORLD TO CONFOUND THE WISE (I Corinthians 1:27).

Together they walked back to the farmer's wife and Monsieur S, who were waiting for them. When Marjorie asked when they wanted to sell, the farmer and his wife said they would sell now, this fall, but they didn't want to move out until spring.

"Next spring is time enough," the woman nodded.

"Yes," Marjorie replied, and silently added, "That is what You told us, Lord!"

"How much do you want for the place?" she asked. They quoted a high price and she smiled. She knew the place would be theirs in God's own time, at the price He had given them, and there was nothing further she could do. Twenty-seven requisites had been met. There simply remained one more—the correct price. Marjorie thanked them and bade them good-bye, saying she would be in touch with them later.

CHAPTER FOURTEEN

Oats, Peas, Beans, and Barley Grow!

Marjorie was ecstatic as she drove back toward town, praising God in song and psalm: I WILL LIFT UP MINE EYES UNTO THE HILLS, FROM WHENCE COMETH MY HELP. MY HELP COMETH FROM THE LORD, WHICH MADE HEAVEN AND EARTH (121:1-2). She admired the beautiful mountains that surrounded the valley and thanked God from the bottom of her heart.

Arriving at the guest house, she asked Madame S if she could stay another night or two.

"Yes, by all means," was the friendly reply. The S's were pleased they could help and were willing to stand kindly by, without question.

Back in Sudbury, the Lord had said that after they moved in the spring and planted their crops, they would want to sell vegetables during the summer, and they might like to have a stand. At least, they should think about how they would sell their produce. Marjorie spent the rest of Saturday looking for a place to build a stand but did not locate one.

That evening another long distance call was made, and Linda and Will heard the good news. What praises and thanksgiving resounded over the phone line as they all rejoiced in the miracles of God and for His goodness—even for Will's tractor! GREAT IS THE LORD, AND GREATLY TO BE PRAISED IN THE CITY OF OUR GOD, IN THE MOUNTAIN OF HIS HOLINESS. BEAUTIFUL FOR SITUATION, THE JOY OF THE WHOLE EARTH, IS MOUNT ZION, ON THE SIDES OF THE NORTH, THE CITY OF THE GREAT KING (Ps. 48:1-2).

Sunday was a restful, beautiful day. After devotions and breakfast, Marjorie leisurely continued her search for a spot that could possibly serve a dual purpose—a vegetable stand and a relaxation area. It could be a place both family and guests could enjoy.

She traveled down the coast toward New Richmond and back to Maria, looking along the water's edge and inquiring. At Maria she found a small cabin on a large corner lot for sale. It was close to the water and faced a side road that led to the center of the village, a short distance away.

In fact, she realized that the lot was only a short walk down the beach from the motel village where they had stayed the night Linda had the vision of "Main Street," the brick Post Office, the valley road, and the river.

A local notary assured her that he could have the papers drawn up by the next evening, and she and the owners could meet at his home in Maria after office hours.

Evening was closing in. After a bite to eat at a wayside restaurant in Maria, Marjorie made her way back to the now familiar guest house in Nouvelle.

Monday dawned bright and cool with a nip of frost in the air. It was a good day to take it easy before the long drive home tomorrow. This was the day she was to sign the papers to buy the seaside lot. She drove down to look it over again.

The road led along the coast of the Baie des Chaleurs, whose water danced with lights as tiny whitecaps rose in response to a salty sea breeze far out in the bay. According to the residents, the summer water here was much warmer than that in Maine or New Hampshire. She believed them, after dipping her finger in. It was truly a sheltered bay of sun-heated water!

The day had grown warmer and the shore was deserted. It was a charming spot and Marjorie spent the day there—walking on the sand, exploring an old mill site, collecting agates, relaxing in the sun, even doing a bit of sketching.

By noon the sea sparkled like a vast mine of sapphires and sea gulls drifted lazily overhead, detached from worldly care. Curled up with a huge log as a backrest, Marjorie drew a blanket snugly around her, read from her Bible, and enjoyed the view. It was a good time to commune with the Lord and thank Him for His great goodness.

Across the bay lay the province of New Brunswick. Far out, Marjorie could see the gap through which the large banana boats and freighters took careful passage through the shoals up into the waters of Campbellton. It was a long way across the blue expanse, and Marjorie had difficulty imagining any part of the salt-water bay frozen in the winter.

The day passed all too swiftly and before she knew it, it was time to meet with the notary. All went like clockwork, and she made her way back to the guest house for her last night.

In the morning after breakfast, Marjorie asked Madame S if it would be possible to stop at the farm and buy a small sack of wheat raised on the property, to take home with her. This had been the Lord's advice that morning, and she, too, thought it was a nice idea. Wheat from the Lord's farm would please Linda and Will immensely. And since Linda was to be their baker, she might want to practice with some blessed grain from the Lord's own acres! Madame S made a phone call and assured Marjorie it would be all right. Thanking the kind and helpful couple and saying a final good-bye, Marjorie departed for the farm.

The farmer and his wife greeted her as she drove in.

"Come in! Come in!" The cordiality of the wife's greeting surprised her! "We want to talk with you."

After they were seated the farmer spoke carefully. "We change our price!" he said, and then quoted the exact price the Lord had specified months before. *"Not a penny less and not a penny more!"*

That very morning the Lord had told her, *"Into thine hand I give thee the promise."* She now understood and humbly believed. In fact, she was delighted to sign papers agreeing to buy the property, pay part of the price that fall, and the remainder in the spring before they moved in. The Lord's work was finished here for the time being. Praise God!

The luminous cloud that had preceded Marjorie's car up to this point floated on ahead and dissolved as she turned south toward Bangor, Maine. Seven hours later, just the right motel room was waiting for her. Another seven-hour drive the next day brought her home to the loving family circle.

The day of Marjorie's return was a time of great rejoicing. Together the threesome knelt in prayer and thanked the Lord for His incomprehensible goodness and love, and for His protecting Spirit that had gone before her, preparing the way, making her journey safe, joyous, and successful.

O COME, LET US SING UNTO THE LORD: LET US MAKE A JOYFUL NOISE TO THE ROCK OF OUR SALVATION (Ps. 95:1).

Of course, one of the first questions Linda and Will asked, after Marjorie had given a detailed account of the trip, was, "When are *we* going to see the place with our own eyes?" In prayer, they were guided to go as soon as possible.

On the weekend of October 27, Will and Linda left Marjorie in charge of their house and children and went to Canada to see for themselves their visions in manifest form. Will couldn't wait to see *his* tractor and Linda was eager to see *her* Post Office and river. They eagerly anticipated a wonderful, though hurried, trip before the snow fell.

When Will and Linda arrived, they were hospitably greeted by the farmer and his wife, who treated them to a delicious noonday meal of homemade soup, liver and onions, potatoes, garden vegetables, and cubed pumpkin in a hot sugar-cinnamon syrup. They say the way to a man's heart is through his stomach, and for Will, it was love at first sight!

It was a great day for all of them as Linda and Will were shown around and saw "with their very own eyes" the wonders the Lord had brought to pass.

Of course they first wanted to see the marvelous tractor and the river—then the other things. They noticed that the farm couple had removed partitions, combining the kitchen, den, and living room. This large room would easily accommodate up to fifty people, a good preparatory step for the new ministry, although it had been done in response to family needs. Families in those parts were large and family life was the hub of activity. Linda and Will could feel a great love as they spoke to others in

95

the area—all kind, family-loving people, respectful toward God and His Son.

Linda and Will covered twelve hundred miles on their visit to the farm. Safely back in Massachusetts Sunday night, Will was ready to go to work the next morning. They shared their precious experience as a threesome and looked to the Lord for further instructions.

During the following weeks, as they prayed and meditated, they continued to receive great inspiration and more instruction. They were told to pray that the people of the world would replace human will with God's will and receive their Savior, Jesus Christ. They were reminded of the first nondenominational Christians, who banded together with one consent and one love of the Lord, without dogma or human doctrine, following only the Lord's commands.

"Thy farm shall be a prayer center for the world, wherein ye all shall have organized prayer times, day and night." They were to establish a community of people interested first and foremost in prayer and Bible meditation.

Besides joining in prayer, everyone was expected to work each morning, helping with farm and household tasks. Afternoons would be spent in Bible study, discussion, and community activities. The Lord, Jesus Christ, emphasized that this was *not* a retirement community.

Each of the three—and others who would permanently join their Canadian work—were to give all their resources to a general fund, out of which community needs would be met. They were to *"charge not"* visitors who came, but let each share whatever they could afford in money, labor, and good will. They were also to keep prayer incessant by dividing assignments among them throughout the day so that prayers would continually flow out to people in need. This is something the threesome have endeavored to do wherever they happen to be. Faithfulness to intercessory prayer is considered the prime function of the founders, and of others who join them.

At their request for instruction, the Lord, in a businesslike manner, dictated a prayer for the world's people, which they were to use daily:

"*May the peace, light, and goodness of God enter the consciousness of man, flood his being, and resurrect the atoms of his thought into the realm of pure Being.*"

There was a second version of the prayer:

"*May the peace, light, and goodness of God enter the consciousness of man, may he be lifted up into the light of Jesus Christ and worship the one true God.*"

He continued to emphasize that their main purpose was to pray for the world, meditate on and understand their Bible, teach, and evolve into the glorious mind and body of Jesus Christ through daily communion. All this was to be done in preparation for His second coming, which they assumed would take place before the year 2000, but the Lord reminded them that OF THAT DAY AND HOUR KNOWETH NO MAN (Matthew 24:36).

CHAPTER FIFTEEN

Exciting Preparations

One morning shortly after their return from Canada, the Lord surprised them: They were to have a building to be used only for prayer and to house the prayer workers. It would be a beautiful white stone temple on the mountainside, dedicated to continuous prayer, day and night. The Lord said that He would call out the workers, who would be 100 percent dedicated to Him.

If until that time the threesome had thought the Lord was fooling around, being lenient, they came to attention and began to work diligently on self-improvement. They began to realize that the work had been launched and that they should prepare themselves as workers in a divine plan, the scope of which they could not even grasp. A thorough overhaul of personality and character began to take place in each of them. The Lord gave constant reminders and helped them improve, always in a constructive love-filled way.

When Will asked if they should take some guns they had inherited from a grandfather's estate, the Lord replied, *"Goest thou thither with me: or goest thou with another?"* A whole explanation followed, but they had gotten the point with the first sentence! The Lord had a way of putting thoughts into a very few words, such as: *"The password is love."* Such a brief statement, but it contained so much!

As Marjorie, Linda, and Will listened, one day Jesus spoke of Himself as a *"Vehicle of devoted purpose,"* bringing all into the Kingdom who would willingly come. However, He would not force anyone against that person's will. The free will of each soul is respected by God. The greatest gift a human being can give to God is his or her will. The Lord had much to say on that subject.

"Now is the day of salvation. Now is the hope of man to choose the

way of good or the way of evil; the way of pleasure or the way of sacrifice; the way of mammon or the way with me."

"O come ye, my beloved children, and walk with me, for what thou givest up is the least of all riches, and my way is fulfilling, with joys everlasting which none shall take away from thee!"

The work on character was important, but there were also physical details that had to be taken care of. Will owned an electric tractor and was thinking of trading it for a Gravely, since that type might be more practical in Canada. What did the Lord think about that, he wanted to know. Will and Linda asked Marjorie to meditate with them about this, and they were soon rewarded.

The Lord encouraged Will in his choice, and even prophesied that the difference in price would be about $100, although Will did not know, at that time, where he would trade. Soon he struck a trade with a local dealer, but the man was unable to follow through, so Will looked around and talked with other dealers. However, he was unable to find one who had the implements he felt they would need. Prices were high, and furthermore, no one particularly wanted what he had to trade.

As time passed, Will became discouraged. "I thought the Lord encouraged me to trade my electric tractor for a Gravely," he grumbled to Marjorie and Linda following another unsuccessful trip in the area. "I've combed this whole eastern area—even the southern part of the state. How are we going to take a garden tractor with us if we can't buy one?"

Linda spoke up. "Do you think for a moment the Lord's hand is shortened? Of course not! He controls all supply, and whatever we need will be forthcoming. I have faith in the Lord, and I am sure He will produce the right machine for us to take to Canada."

They again asked the Lord about the tractor, and He replied that there was a Gravely dealer to the west of them still uncontacted, who had just the right trade at the difference in price He had originally quoted. The threesome got out the map and selected several large cities in western Massachusetts, and from a Gravely sales listing, Will found a dealer to contact. The man had exactly what Will wanted, was delighted to take the electric tractor in trade—and the difference in price was exactly $100!

At the Lord's instruction, the threesome obediently applied for Canadian residency. They were kindly told by the official in charge that even after they filed their papers and had an interview, it would take some time to process such a request. In time, they would receive an official decision from the Canadian government. They might be accepted or they might be refused. The officer could not promise anything.

The Lord, on the other hand, promised everything! He assured them they would be accepted, because He had already planned the whole thing. *"So be prepared to move at a certain time in the spring!"* Along with this assurance came a barrage of daily instruction in everything from explanations of biblical passages to attitudes, emotions, reactions, conscience, fasting, food, love, enlightenment, freedom, death, and life.

He instructed humankind how to live morally and harmoniously: Love, applied daily, brings provision and true peace. In fact, there was no reason the threesome could not develop their own little heaven on earth, for He was sending them to *"holy ground"*.

In meditation, they received that they would, in time, be joined by others who had concern for the welfare of the world—people who would love farming and would join in supporting the group through their combined talents. They were not to worry about supply. To their inquiry about income, He replied that they were to earn it through their crops, animals, milk, wool, crafts, and by working for others, using their skills and abilities.

The threesome began to dispose of unnecessary items and purchase needed ones. A huge trailer truck arrived one day with a large grain mill Marjorie had ordered. It was stored in the front hall until moving day. Linda bought heavy-duty ski suits for the children and began packing dishes. Will gathered his tools, to decide what to take and what to leave behind. (They had been liberally strewn across the estate, so it took some time to locate them all.) And what about their cars? Would they need both? And if one were to be sold, *which* one? Should Marjorie part with her pet white Chrysler? Or should Will part with the best car he had ever owned—the new Dodge? Both were owned clear and free, so they decided to ask the Lord. After all, He was Lord over cars as well as people. Didn't He own everything in the world?

They were due for another surprise! They were to sell both their cars, pool their money, and buy a good used family car and a tough truck with a detachable camper top! How about that? The Lord was a practical Lord as well as a Lord of love. THE LORD IS GOOD; HIS MERCY IS EVERLASTING (Ps. 100:5).

It was not without some human trepidation that they parted with their automobiles, which meant there was still a residue of human desire left. Marjorie had a lump in her throat as the new owner drove her white convertible away, never to be seen again! Linda and Will also parted sadly with their Dodge, but they all had resolved to take up their crosses and follow wherever the Lord might lead them, and they knew this was the right thing to do.

A good used, economically priced Plymouth soon went on sale. They bought it, and Will happily put in his order for a green and white truck with four-wheel drive. Now that the switch had been made, they could feel order taking place in their affairs, and they all felt good about that! But they still weren't sure Canada would accept them!

The Lord gave them specific instructions for use of each room in their new house. The upper part of the extension (where the farmer's wife used to hang her laundry) was to be made into a chapel for prayer and Bible meditation. They were to change the location of the cellar entrance: The trap door in the middle of the kitchen floor was to be closed off and a full set of stairs added to another spot. A space was designated in the outer shed for tools. The Lord had His set of plans, all based on order and these were shared daily with the threesome.

Things moved rapidly as November passed. The move presented many challenges, as well as many opportunities. When should Marjorie and Will resign their positions? What should they tell people? They had no way of knowing what their new life would entail. Would they need Marjorie's fine china service for twelve, or her antique glassware and china, or should it all be sold and the money put into the pot? What books should they study or take?

Marjorie felt led to sell her glassware and antique china, but she gave her large service to her younger daughter, along with the family silverware. Will was to read everything he could find about agriculture and raising sheep and goats. Linda was to learn about cheese and butter making, yeast, and the dyeing of wool—and even how to build a fire in a wood stove. It was a time of intense learning, with gales of laughter as they made humorous discoveries.

During quiet times, beautiful inspiration filtered in. At one time Marjorie received detailed instructions which clarified the Ten Commandments, and which they studied with eagerness and interest. The instructions were full of practical advice they would need in daily living at their prayer community: love of the Lord, obedience to the will of the Father, and the brotherhood of man.

CHAPTER SIXTEEN

Off to Israel

The Lord continued to speak of northward and east, and urged them to pack and prepare themselves—*"for that day soon cometh when ye shall depart bag and baggage!"* Yes, He insisted, they should finish packing and set their house in order so that they could go to Israel!

"Israel!" Will and Linda and Marjorie echoed. "How soon, with whom, and why?" A hundred questions arose. They had just been complaining because there weren't enough hours in the day to accomplish all they thought they should do! (They had no idea what tireless workers they would become as the Lord strode swiftly ahead, clearing the way!)

He told them they should familiarize themselves with His native land, visit the places He had trod. He wanted them to have the beautiful experience of seeing His Holy Land. And He added that it was much like the new land He was sending them to—the land He had *"prepared for you northward and east."*

Excitedly, they procured brochures and found that the World Bible Conference was taking place in Israel in March. The tour was scheduled to leave Kennedy Airport in New York on March 6 and would return on March 14. Their brains whirled. Would they have sufficient time to do everything that still needed to be done, if they took time off to go to Israel?

The intellect again was trying to interfere with divine guidance, but they caught it this time. Disposing of questions, they accepted the Lord's word that they should go to Israel, knowing that somehow everything that needed to be done would be done before March 6, and that the right person or persons would be available to take care of the children and household in their absence. Faith was removing mountains!

Christmas came, a precious time of devotion and celebration, perhaps the last in their native land. But melancholy departed when they thought of the valley beautiful and the work they would soon be doing for their Lord and their God.

During this time of planning, packing, and preparation, Linda continued to give music lessons to her fifteen students, but planned to discontinue soon in order to be ready to leave for Israel. Will worked daily in the greenhouses, while Marjorie gradually tapered off her classes and ministry. Her faithful church members wished to continue and accepted a new leader of her choice. She finished packing her household things and turned her attention to helping Linda.

About mid-January, they were informed that the Hotel Diplomat had been engaged to house the Bible Conference delegates. A special 747 Jumbo Jet from Israel's El Al Airlines had been assigned for conference use and was scheduled to fly nonstop from New York to Tel Aviv in ten and a half hours. Delegates, including groups of ministers and evangelists, would be going from North America and several foreign countries. The purpose of the World Bible Conference was to bring together, in an international forum, authoritative leaders in the relevant fields of biblical interest. There would be special services, featuring some of the world's outstanding preachers, teachers, and musicians. Marjorie was pleased to receive an invitation to address the assembly in Cana of Galilee, where Christ had performed His first miracle, turning water into wine at the wedding feast.

By mid-February they had received their final communications from the tour director, together with tickets, packets of documents, maps, baggage tags, and itinerary. The Lord also told them many beautiful things about His land that He wanted them to especially notice and enjoy—and they were to be sure to take note of *one man* who would become an *important* friend over the following years. They wondered who it would be and what he would do that would be so important for their ministry. Needless to say, the threesome was excited as the day of departure arrived!

This was no time to slow down! The pace increased as March approached. There was much more packing and sorting yet to be done before they could leave for Canada.

A kind relative arrived to take over and see the threesome off to Boston, where they took the train to New York and boarded the big 747 with a mass of friendly people — in all, there were about 400 people aboard. El Al Airline was using the Air France terminal, and although the plane was scheduled to depart at 8:30 P.M., it did not leave until much later. It was close to midnight before dinner was served, and then they learned that the course of their flight must be altered. Because of danger of being shot down over the Mediterranean, they would fly first to London to refuel, and then overland to Tel Aviv, avoiding France because of an air traffic controllers' strike. The flight took twenty-four hours instead of the ten and a half scheduled.

Weary from the long flight, they all arrived at the hotel in Jerusalem ready for a good night's sleep. But the city was over-crowded with visitors, and somehow Marjorie's reservation was missing — she had no room! Will and Linda however, invited her to share theirs while they were in Jerusalem.

The following few days unfolded quickly, with visits to the garden tomb at Gethsemane, the Mt. of Olives, Hebrew University, Nazareth, Cana, Mt. Tabor, Megiddo, Capernaum, the Mt. of Beatitudes, Bethlehem, Jericho, the Qumran Caves, and Galilee. There, they crossed the Sea of Galilee to reenact the feeding of the five thousand on the opposite shore.

As the threesome saw the small amount of St. Peter's fish and bread and the large number of conference members, Marjorie remarked that a major miracle *had* to take place! And it did! As she and the other ministers came forward to bless and break the bread and fish, giving them out on special commemorative plates, neither bread nor fish failed. There was enough for all, and some left over!

Event after event was prayerfully entered into and the Holy Spirit was overwhelmingly present. Behind the scenes, though, there was a feeling of tension in the land. They passed tanks parked beside the roads and noticed wire strung up here and there. The

The threesome in Israel

sound of a bomb interrupted one of the programs. Yet no one allowed this feeling of uneasiness to interfere with the richness of the program and the beauty of the experience. The request of a three-day extension of their visas, however, was denied.

They made many friends, but no one man in particular seemed to relate unduly to their ministry. The threesome wondered who the special one was who would be so important to them. Had they misinterpreted what the Lord had told them, or would the man show up later? If so, what would be his purpose?

They had faithfully risen early to maintain their times apart with their Lord in prayer, and it had paid rich dividends. One morning in Jerusalem, Marjorie was shown in vision a room whose plain stonelike walls were highly polished, as was its floor.

"What is this?" Marjorie asked the Lord. "Oh," she observed, "It must be a room in a museum somewhere." Then the Lord directed her attention onto the floor, where she saw gifts and a container of incense. The Lord gave her to understand that this was the room called the Holy of Holies, part of the temple that would later be built in Jerusalem. In this room the image of the beast (Antichrist) would be set up. The image would be able to move and speak, and it would be worshiped by the people of the world as God. *"Do not accept his mark on your body,"* Jesus Christ warned.

Searching their Bibles, the threesome found reference to this in Jesus' words in Matthew 24:15-21, in Revelation 13:5,6,15,16,17, and also in the Old Testament in Daniel 11:21, as well as other places.

CHAPTER SEVENTEEN

The Pass Over

The return home from Israel was uneventful. The threesome barely had time to assess the trip and take a second breath when they heard from the Canadian consulate that their request for residency had been granted. Their legal documents arrived. With this, the Lord advised Marjorie and Will to go to Canada and complete the purchase of the property. Also, they were to order the moving van for April 17. They did this without delay, for they were learning that their Lord was not only a Lord of great love and compassion—the perfect teacher and director—but an excellent business manager!

The remaining days before the move were extremely busy. Will and Marjorie left shortly for Canada to complete the papers, to get some soil samples, for testing, and to worship on the temple site. Their arrival was expected by the owners, who gladly received them as house guests.

Will was surprised to find so much snow still on the land. He and Marjorie wondered how they would dig in the frozen ground for the soil samples, and how they would get up the mountainside to the temple site. But the owners' snowmobile was brought out, and Will and Marjorie flew over the snow-laden land for their first winter devotions on the mountainside.

It was a glorious day. The sun was dazzling on the snow and the air sparkled with crystal cleanness. It was April 1, 1973, a Sunday, and they had obeyed their Lord: "Go ye unto thy high mount of prayer, then meditate on my word and be at peace." Marjorie pulled a small Bible out of her jacket pocket as they reached the place of prayer, where the forest began above the cleared mountainside.

The view was breathtaking! They looked down and across the crystal snow upon the valley beautiful and the purple mountainsides, so much like those they had seen in the Lord's Holy Land. To the left stretched the sea, and overhead circled an occasional gull. High up on the rocky ledges a hawk was calling. Otherwise, it was perfectly still.

WORSHIP THE LORD IN THE BEAUTY OF HOLINESS! (1 Chronicles 16:29c), they read aloud. BE STILL, AND KNOW THAT I AM GOD! (Ps. 46:10). Oh, the beauty of these biblical passages they loved so well, and the loveliness of the scene that lay before them! And to think, it all belonged to the Lord, and He would permit them to use His land and to live in this valley beautiful! Their eyes filled with tears of gladness. God was so good!

After voicing prayers for the people of the world in unison, they became still and listened to the Lord, absorbing His light and peace. His Presence was tremendously real. They felt His anointing upon this place where later would rise the beautiful white-stone Prayer Temple. They could not help giving thanks for the prayer workers who would dwell in their beautiful temple, serving the Lord day and night; God's Holy Spirit fell upon Will and Marjorie as they voiced praises to His holy name!

Reluctantly they left the temple site and mounted the snowmobile. Down they went to the fence line. Will tried to maneuver around it, but—Whoops!—over they went into a drift, with snow up to their hips! It was a difficult trick to climb aboard again, but they finally managed and continued down the steep passage, across the spacious fields of shining white, down again and across the frozen brook, then across more fields to the farmhouse.

The warm fire in the kitchen stove felt good as they backed up to it to thaw out. The aroma of meat pie with fresh-cooked vegetables filled the room. It was a dinner fit for a king. Marjorie and Will were most grateful to their new Canadian friends.

It was a quick weekend trip, but all was accomplished—the final purchase, the deed, and so on. Everyone was satisfied, and Will and Marjorie returned to the States.

Then there was a constant surge of activity—last-minute dental appointments, slipcovers for a couch and chair, refinishing for an antique table, rugs to be cleaned, draperies to be bought. All this, along with the many other items that had to be either bought or packed, plus caring for the children and the details of daily living left little time. Friends and relatives stopped in to make last calls. A few people came out of curiosity, to find out what was going on. Seekers of the Lord called or visited. Some came for healing prayer or light on the Bible. All in all, it was a busy time until April 17, when the moving van pulled into the yard.

The day began as usual with 5:00 A.M. prayers, Bible reading, and meditation. After breakfast the movers arrived. Since Will and Linda were still not entirely packed, the men loaded Marjorie's things first, and then the things from Linda's first and second floors, while Marjorie helped her continue to pack the goods from the attic and basement. This was North American's largest van, and it took the movers all day to pack it. But it was not large enough! The driver had to call the company for another smaller van, which arrived the next morning, and not until 4:00 P.M. that day was the house finally empty and clean. After a brief sad good-bye to Will's folks, the family followed the two vans out of the yard, Will driving his new truck with Sparkie on the seat beside him, and Marjorie in line behind him, driving the family car with Linda and the children. The new truck held close to four thousand pounds of tools and farm machinery, and Marjorie's car was loaded to the roof.

They had agreed to meet the big van at the Canadian border at 8:00 A.M. the next morning, thinking that would give them plenty of time. But it was spring in the northland. Although the roads in the States were free of snow, there were frost heaves in the least expected places!

They had invested in a snow plow that attached to the truck. The dealer who sold them the plow advised Will not to leave the hydraulic pump hooked up during the long trip, since he would be driving for quite a distance at high speeds. The plow was held up by a heavy chain in front of the radiator. Every time Will hit a large bump, the plow would be tossed up and the chain holding it would release, allowing it to drop to the ground. Each time this happened Will had to stop, attach the chain, and raise the plow again. This operation took half an hour each time.

After several such incidents, Will finally found an old coat hanger and wired the chain so that it couldn't come off its hook. Beside this problem, Will had another! Since the snow plow was in front of the radiator, it allowed very little air to enter, so although the temperature outside was around 50° the truck would overheat. Will not only had to stop occasionally to let it cool, he also had to drive with all the windows open because the cab was roasting hot inside. Each time Will stopped, everyone prayed—frost heaves and trucks have never had so much prayer, before or since!

During the slow, tedious trek the vans had long since disappeared, and all too soon, night was upon the family. They ate sandwiches as they drove and pressed on. Ordinarily, it would have taken them seven hours to reach the border, but at the rate they were traveling, it looked as though it would take a good fourteen hours.

At 3:00 A.M. the next morning, everyone was exhausted. At Houlton, Maine, they rented a motel unit, sleep soundly for three hours, then got up and drove on. Daylight was fast approaching, but fortunately, the big van had come over the same road, so it had traveled slowly also. At 9:30 on the morning of April 19, 1973, the truck with Will and Sparkie and the car with Marjorie and the family arrived in Van Buren, Maine, and crossed over the St. John River into Canada. And the big van had not yet arrived! They had time to process their many papers and get ready before it came into sight, a half hour later. They learned that the smaller van had put the rest of their things in storage and would bring them later.

The Canadian officials were courteous and helpful. Finding everything in good order, they passed the van through customs, and the caravan traveled on. On this special day, April 19, Marjorie had read aloud from the Bible while Linda drove. They had prayed as usual for the world's people, and then the Lord's message was given to them: "Go forth then this day with joyous hearts for thy pilgrimage is thy passing over into thy promised land which my people, the Jews, were celebrating the day thy movers began thy moving. Rejoice now, for thy new life lies ahead for thee, foursquare and deep."

They had thought the Maine roads had bad frost heaves, but they decided they may have been mistaken. Canadian Route 17, from St. Leonard to Campbellton, New Brunswick, was so bloated they had to creep along very slowly, not only so as not to lose the snow plow, but so as not to lose the entire load! From time to time they stopped and one of the children would ride in the truck. This gave the family a little variety and helped to keep the children interested.

At about 4:00 P.M., just three minutes behind the van, the family drove up the road to their new home. As they did so, a great multitude of snow-white birds rose like a cloud off the roof of the farmhouse and flew away. They were birds about the size of doves, but no one could identify them. It was a beautiful and unusual welcome. Through the years that passed, the birds were never seen again.

As Joe, the driver of the van, and his two helpers walked to greet them, they all jumped joyfully out of the cars, stretching their legs and hugging one another. They were so happy! Everyone helped the movers unload the things that would be needed for the night. It was late and everyone was hungry, so they all went to the nearest restaurant, fifteen miles away, for a delicious supper.

Unfortunately, unknown to them, there had been a misunderstanding about their arrival time, and the former owners had expected them the day before. A nice dinner had been prepared to welcome them, but since they did not arrive that day, Monsieur and Madame had left for their new home in the village.

That night, sleeping accommodations were hastily prepared in the farmhouse and the children tumbled wearily into bed. The threesome held their evening prayers, and the Lord blessed them: *"For ye three wast called and did respond. Ye came to ye knew not what! But ye came! And now I do bless thee."*

The next morning they held prayers in the second-floor guest room which they chose to use as their prayer room until the chapel was ready. The movers returned and now began to unload in earnest. Before long, boxes filled the kitchen, the library, the upstairs rooms, and the shed area, as well as the main part of the big barn and grain shed. At last the truck was empty.

Breathing a big sigh of relief, Joe leaned against the sink with a tall glass of cold water.

He asked Will, "How did you folks happen to move way up here, anyway?"

While Linda mixed up a batch of pancakes and the coffee began to perk, Will shared some of the reasons they had moved. The questions came flying as the three men wanted to know more about God and how He was dealing with people in these days.

"I thought God was off in the sky somewhere," Joe commented, after Will told how they had been guided in prayer and meditation to seek the Lord's will for their lives and how the Lord had directed them in finding the farm.

After listening intently to the discussion, one of the young helpers remarked, "If it was important for you to know the Lord's will for you, then perhaps I should learn how to meditate and find out what God wants me to do."

"That's right," Linda affirmed. "You can see that these are days of great change, and He needs helpers of all kinds. This does not necessarily mean that everyone has to move in order to serve the Lord, but it does mean that everyone should accept their Savior, Jesus Christ, that He is present in His Spirit and needs everyone who is willing to help Him."

As the movers prepared to depart, the family prayed for their safe journey and for their closer walk with Jesus Christ in the days ahead.

Later on that day, a beautiful rainbow arched over the end of their valley near the sea. The rainbow of God's promise was dear to their hearts, for He had told them He would enter into a covenant with them. If they would go and do as He told them, He in turn would always protect and provide for them. And so their first rainbow symbolized their covenant with the Lord, Jesus Christ, sealing their promise to be faithful to the end of their days.

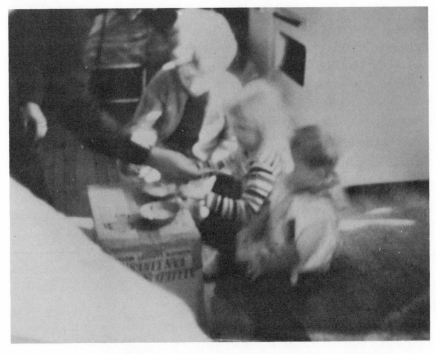

Will and Linda feeding Betsy and Ben on top of packing boxes

CHAPTER EIGHTEEN

Getting Our Bearings

View from the Temple site

The next few days were spent walking around and trying to get their bearings. The children ate on packing boxes and thought the picnic great fun, but the adults soon became frustrated, looking for things that were "in a box" somewhere in the sea of boxes!

The third day after their "passover" was Easter Sunday, April 22, a glorious, clear, sunny day. What a good time to celebrate by going up to the temple site! Although there was still deep snow on the ground (drifts two to three feet deep), they hiked up the mountainside, taking turns carrying Benjamin, who was too small to make it on his own. Sparkie frolicked beside them, running his nose through the snow and butting into Ben, who thought it was very funny. After more than an hour's climb, they reached the site and settled down for devotions.

As the five of them viewed the valley from above, they were filled with wonder at its size and beauty. Little Betsy remarked how pretty it was. They sang and read from the Bible, took Communion, then meditated quietly on God's Holy Word. They thanked the Lord for His resurrection and for their safe arrival and their new life's work.

The Lord told the threesome that as they crossed out their negatives and let *Him* free their thoughts for new, joyous, positive Christed ones, they were still working at their "passover." BE RENEWED IN THE SPIRIT OF YOUR MIND! (Ephesians 4:23).

He reminded them that He was their resurrection and that as He lived in them, and they *allowed* Him to cleanse their emotions and attitudes, that was, in a sense, freedom from the grave. In Jesus Christ, they had new life! They were excited and happy! This was a heaven on earth—they could hardly wait for the Lord's coming to take them into an even more glorious Kingdom! This simple occasion held a spirit of holiness that has never let them go. The awe and wonder of their work has lasted through the years.

One of the Lord's first instructions after their arrival directed them to print a newsletter to send to their friends. Marjorie had previously sent out a little flier to her congregation from time to time, so she offered to be responsible for the newsletter, with the help of the other two.

Clearing a space in what would be the family room, Will set their little printing machine on top of some boxes, and there Marjorie ran off the stencils she had cut on a portable typewriter. The print was not very clear—her good typewriter was still "in a box" somewhere—but it was legible. Here is part of their first monthly periodical, which they named the *Messenger*, giving a first-hand report of their journey.

Box 8, Nouvelle Ouest, Quebec, Canada GOC 2GO May 4, 1973

MESSAGE FROM REV. MARJORIE

Greetings from Nouvelle Ouest, Canada! This is to let you know where I am and what I am doing.

The Lord has given us a wonderful new ministry here of prayer for the world, and Will and Linda Hawes, my son-in-law and daughter, have been commissioned to minister with me. Their two children Betsy, age 7, and Benjamin, age 2, are with us, and our joint ministry is off to a wonderful start! The Holy Spirit is a tremendous moving factor in our lives and we experience fresh inspiration daily.

On April 19th we arrived at our new home in Nouvelle Ouest by 4 PM just three minutes after the van arrived. You can imagine our awe and amazement upon seeing 60 to 70 birds fly from our house to greet us!

Three days later on Easter Sunday we hiked through some snow to our mountainside where the Lord has told us we will eventually erect a beautiful Prayer Temple. To sit on that hillside and look down the slopes across to the lovely mountains rimming the valley and to feel the Lord's sweet peace and serenity is quite an experience. We blessed and broke bread there, holding communion with the Lord in the sunshine and clear, sparkling air. The Lord is most powerfully present daily, and from that day on we have kept a prayer vigil hourly for the people of the United States, Canada and the world.

Although every room in the house and part of the barn and sheds are filled with boxes, we are working diligently to set all in order. One of the guest rooms was quickly settled and set aside for prayer. We seem to have many prayer partners here! This past Sunday we were all in that room for our morning devotions when about 40 birds alighted in the apple tree outside our window. The interesting part was that they were all perched *facing* us and SINGING their hearts out in praise to their Creator.

From the inception of this prayer ministry miracle has followed miracle and they never cease to manifest!

LINES FROM LINDA

The Lord has directed us all the way!

We arrived in Nouvelle West, our new home, at 4 PM and prepared to unload. It was then we discovered that the movers demanded cash, not a check, before they would unload a single item. Banking doors were closed and little did we realize at those tired, dusk hours how the Lord's hand was at work in our behalf! Will, Mother and I opened our wallets, never having planned on retaining cash enough for our van expense and found not only the sum to pay the estimate, but enough and more to pay the complete bill.

The following day, after a good night's sleep in our own beds, in our own

117

home, we were told by neighbors that NO BANKS were open that day, Good Friday, or Saturday, because churches were holding services through Easter Sunday and through Monday, and a legal holiday had been declared. This would have meant all our shipment would have gone to Rimouski (some 200 miles above us on the opposite side of the Gaspé) to be stored for the long weekend. Extra expense such as storage fees, loading and unloading fees, would have been added, *plus* the inconvenience of our lodging in a motel for the long Easter weekend. This is only a few of the ways the Lord has worked in our behalf.

In a couple of weeks the land will be plowed, and wheat, oats, rye, and barley will be sown, together with vegetables. Our raspberry plants arrived yesterday. Reaping and harvesting will yield plenteous crops, for we plan to use those protein grains in our cooking. Our mill will be grinding forth our grain.

WORDS FROM WILL

We are in a primarily French speaking community and the other day I started off to conduct some business. I stopped by the building site of a friend of mine. A retired gentleman was also looking at the cellar hole, wishing that he had something to do. Now this particular man speaks both French and English very well and accompanied me happily for the entire afternoon and interpreted for me and showed me around.

God filled my need before I even knew I had a need. Believe me, if it hadn't been for him I would have had great difficulty accomplishing my tasks. I have come to know through daily prayer and meditation, *God is Real! God is Good!* God is the *only* answer to the world's problems.

BETSY'S LOVE CORNER was also started and continued through the years until she left for college: "I am having a good time in school and I am learning some French words. I have three friends who speak a little English, but mostly French. I had a birthday party last night. I have three cats. They love to play in the barn. One is Stripe-tail, one is Black-paws, and one is White-paws. Love, Betsy."

The question of where Betsy would go to school had presented itself upon their arrival. Should she go to a French or to an English-speaking school? Seeking the Lord's help, they received *"Allow her this opportunity to learn the French language fluently. This will be a prime asset for life. . . . Language learning is vital to thy welfare."*

Betsy found it difficult to cope in a totally French-speaking school. It took her about a year to master the situation, but since then she had become fluent in the language. She used it as a minor in college—and also as a valuable skill for earning part of her expenses through her ability to translate.

However, Marjorie, Will, and Linda all had difficulty understanding anything that was said to them. All the neighbors spoke such rapid French!

One day Will needed some assistance and caught up with a neighbor walking down the road. Linda and Marjorie, watching from the window, sympathized with him as he motioned and waved his arms, trying in sign language to get his message across. Finally, the neighbor, who must have been anguishing for Will, said, "O.K.," and continued the conversation in English!

Other kind folk in the area made frequent friendly calls on the new family, always bringing a jar of preserves, a cake, pie, or whatever came to hand. They were sympathetic with the family's inability to converse in French, and tried to help. This attitude was greatly appreciated.

One evening a couple of men stopped in to talk to Will and politely spoke with Linda and Marjorie. Marjorie tried to use her best French, but after they left, Will said, grinning, "Do you realize you just asked Mr. Thibault how much his wife was?"

When an English couple visited the man told Marjorie of the severe winters and jokingly warned her that the snow often came up to the second-story windows. He inquired whether they had brought snowshoes, for they would need them to get out of the house. After the couple left, she quickly found Linda and Will to warn them of the terrible winters. How the visitors must have chuckled over Marjorie's acceptance of their fabricated story!

Meanwhile, Linda was quickly learning the new language. She welcomed visitors and chatted amiably, enjoying everyone who came along.

It was an intensive time of adjustment for the family as they learned, first of all, how to live together harmoniously in a totally new environment; second, how to find their own niches of service in the new framework; third, how to let the Lord do all their thinking, feeling, speaking and acting; and fourth, how to cope with a new language.

CHAPTER NINETEEN

Visitors Begin

Visitors help us tap water from the earth's "fountains".

If they had wondered whether the Lord was sending them to the end of the world and thought they would never have visitors, they were mistaken. From the very beginning, visitors began coming from the United States, and even from England. They walked between the piles of boxes, helped here and there, dicussed the truths of God, received prayers and divine healing.

There were not a lot of visitors at one time—just one or two or a family now and then—but the flow was continuous through the years that followed. The first arrived from Vermont on June 17 and stayed for a week. During the course of that time they not only studied the Bible and prayed, but helped Will drive a well-point ten feet into the earth, where they struck water. After screwing a pumphead onto the pipe, they pumped until the water was clear. And when it was sampled, it was *good water!*

By this time the garden spots had been chosen and four gardens planted. The pump water was plenteous enough to take care of the closest garden all summer, when it was hot and dry with temperatures ranging in the 90s.

The Vermont guests caught the spirit of the ministry and decided they would join the threesome in prayer when they reached home. They wrote, "This is a wonderful venture and a great need in a troubled world. Love alone is life! It was a wonderful week!"

One afternoon shortly afterward the threesome witnessed one of the most beautiful rainbows they had ever seen. It was double and brilliant, stretching across the entire valley. Oddly, both ends seemed to touch the earth. Forest and mountain were almost blocked out by the vibrant colors. One end of the bow touched down at the site of the Prayer Temple; the other entered the neighbor's field.

By late June 1973, when blue and white weather in the 90s had arrived, Will decided to tackle the renovation of the prayer chapel. Slowly and cautiously he gathered the supplies he needed and began work on the attic of the old shed. This was something entirely new to him, as he had not built anything before in his entire life—but he was willing to try! When he got stuck and didn't have a clue as to how to proceed, he would sit down in the sawdust and commune with the Lord. He found that the Lord was really a very good carpenter! He never let him down.

Will decided to leave the ladderlike stairs in for the time being, thus providing a way for the family to climb up into the still unfinished area to hold their morning and evening devotions. The prayer chapel became a place of spiritual refuge over the years, as they faced various issues and prayed their way through. The Lord was always there to meet and pray with them, and to guide and help them in any way that was needed. One day Linda, trying to locate her two missing children, found them up in the chapel, holding their own prayer service.

As the three began to settle in and learn more about the community, they discovered that a ferryboat crossed the Baie des Chaleurs from Dalhousie, on the New Brunswick side, to Miguasha, on the outskirts of their own town. This provided interesting transportation for their guests. There was also an airport at Charlo, a couple of miles above Dalhousie. People could fly in, take a taxi to the ferry, and cross to Miguasha on the Quebec side, where they could be picked up. Along the shore near the ferryboat landing was a cluster of summer and year-round cottages with a magnificent view of the blue bay. The ferry is no longer in operation and today it is an eighty-mile round trip to the airport by car.

The airport and ferry, together with the fine overnight train service between Nouvelle and Montreal, were real blessings. They had no idea that their location, even in a rural out-of-the-way section, would be blessed with these services. There were also buses that ran twice a day.

The threesome had been told by the Lord that love was to be expressed to one and all, no matter who, or what the conditions. Many people came, and they all needed and wanted love—God's love—and Marjorie, Will, and Linda had opportunities again and again to give and share that perfect love. Love, a disciplined way of life, was emphasized.

It was no problem to feed people in the summertime. Gardening was a necessity and also a joy. But Linda also wanted a source of good milk, and this desire was soon fulfilled by a white milk truck that drove into the yard. A farmer's son, Tim, drove the truck, delivering milk in his starched white uniform. Tim was a gentle, kind young man, tall, slender, and tanned, with an outdoor look.

Not only were the children delighted with the milk, but the barn cats loved it also. When the family bought the farm the cats were included. There had been two—Mama cat and Blackie. Mama was a salt-and-pepper cat, small and wiry. Blackie was a huge, powerful male who could catch and kill the largest rat that dared show up. A third cat, a stray, had moved in, and Mama was soon known as Boss Cat.

The former owners told the family that Mama cat was barren, had never had kittens, was quite old and might die soon, so it would be best to keep the stray that had appeared. Mama cat ran wildly for her life whenever she saw a human being, as did Blackie and the stray. But the family decided to make friends with them. Gradually, as they were fed the milk, which the former owners had always left them alone to drink, the family began to pray for them and talk to them, and tried to pat them.

Mama Boss Cat and a stray

It was about a year before Mama Boss Cat would allow herself to be patted, but then she began to purr enthusiastically, showing her pleasure. But when her pleasure reached the boiling point, one needed to watch out, because she would suddenly reach out and cuff the patter!

Only a short year afterward, Mama Boss Cat became pregnant and gave birth to two cute kittens. This continued for many years; Mama cat became Grandma and Great-grandma. At the time of this writing, twelve years have passed, and Mama is still alive and Boss Cat today.

But the children and barn cats did not get all the milk Tim delivered. Linda saved much to make bread. She visited her neighbors to watch and learn, and went home to develop her skill. With weekly practice she soon grew expert, and the aroma of baking bread became a new part of the family tradition. Not only did she make wheat bread, but she sought out recipes for other grain mixtures.

One night the family got to bed late, and as a consequence, everyone was very sleepy the next morning. Since Tim was used to stepping into the kitchen to deliver the milk, they made a special effort this morning to be up early as usual to greet him.

Marjorie was in her robe, washing breakfast dishes, when Linda dragged downstairs as though walking in her sleep, staggered to a chair, and grabbed a blanket that happened to be lying there. She wrapped herself in it, sank in a heap on the rug, and went back to sleep, submerged in the blanket.

Soon Tim bolted in the door, shining bright in his starched white uniform, with a bottle of milk clutched in each hand. Smiling, he held them out for Marjorie to take so that he could pass in the other bottles. About that time, Linda, hearing the commotion, roused with a groan and yawn, rising up from within the mass of blanket on the floor. Tim stared at the moving, groaning blanket. His hair rose, and he shouted, "Mon Dieu!"

Marjorie grabbed the bottles of milk as they were about to slip from his startled hands, and Linda emerged sleepily to say hello. To say their greeting that morning was a bit unorthodox would be an exaggeration!

The family enjoyed taking visitors up to the deserted colony site, past the waterfalls and chasm, through the densely forested cliffs, up to the open sky and bare, brown fields of the mountaintop. Or they might go to look for agates on the shore, or down to their Maria beach property. It was a joy to lie on the sand and share thoughts of God, or walk quietly along the shore as the water softly lapped the beach. At eventide they often built a fire from driftwood, cooked supper, sang, and had another time of sharing as the sun dipped slowly in the west.

Because of the numerous settling-in activities, the gardens were planted late. When Will asked if he should take a chance and plant anyway, the Lord responded with some good instructions about chance-taking: *"Chance is the mistress of fate—and fate bringeth all to the grave."* Rather than believing in chance, they were to *bless* their seed, *plant*, and *expect* good results. That was the way the Lord expected His work to be run—whether it was actual seed to be planted in the ground, or seed thoughts from biblical inspiration planted in the heart of a seeker. *"If you never plant, you will never reap!"* He told them.

The gardens grew that year. The seed was blessed, the weather perfect, with hot sun in the daytime and soft rain at night. Everyone in the valley remarked about the good weather that year. How the Lord blessed everyone's gardens!

One day after the first visitors had left, Marjorie, returning from a trip to Campbellton, drove past a hitchhiker. As she continued on her way, the Lord called her attention to the man and told her she had been wrong to pass that particular person without giving him a ride. It was not her practice to pick up hitchhikers but the Lord said this one was O.K. She stopped and backed up until he could climb into the back seat. He had a large bag and a guitar, and was glad for the lift.

They began to talk, and Marjorie was led to tell him something about why she and her family lived there. When she invited him to their farm, he accepted reluctantly, saying he was on his way to a friend's home quite a distance away and had hoped to make it by evening. However, he was fascinated with her story and decided he would like to meet the rest of the family.

When they drove in, Will and Linda had just finished watering the fifty strawberry plants Marjorie had set out the day before. The hitchhiker, Vic, enjoyed their companionship so much that he accepted their invitation to stay for dinner and overnight, then helped Will with the chores and entered into devotions. The next morning he insisted on working with Will in the field to repay his night's lodging. Before leaving, he got out his guitar and gave a little concert in gratitude for the family's hospitality.

The note he left in his room was touching: "Winding up here was an unexpected, yet enlightening experience! . . . It's been a long time since I met a family so dedicated to living a Christian life of love. . . . I'll bet your thing here will grow. It's been an overnight stay I won't forget." Many years have passed since Vic walked out of their yard. But when the Holy Spirit of God touches a person, can they ever forget?

Several single friends and a couple of families from the United States came and went during the summer months. Departing guests made numerous references to the valley as one of the most beautiful places on earth and said they felt "privileged to have been a part of a community guided by God." They were sure it would "play an important role in the future for the well-being and uplifting of a great many people in this world."

Not all their ministering was done in Canada, however. July of that year found Marjorie on a field trip, speaking in Miami, Florida.

CHAPTER TWENTY

Mission to Great Britain

As the summer days passed and the guests shared, the Lord instructed the family to consider ministering in Great Britain soon—possibly in November. Everyone, children included, was to go. The adults were to earn their own way. In the meantime, they should think about building a storehouse. Possibly they should have someone dig and cement the cellar for it before they left. As for the farm, the Lord promised He had in mind a proper caretaker for the farm in their absence, and He directed them to a family which gladly accepted the opportunity.

As Linda had been playing her beautiful new piano that summer, groups of young people walking past heard her music and had expressed a desire to take lessons. As a result, she had found herself in business and already had earned part of what would be needed for her ticket! Marjorie had enough for her expenses, but Will had no idea how he would raise his funds. His only experience had been in greenhouse work and there were no such openings in that area.

It was decided they would depart on November 6 and return December 10. That would give Marjorie enough time to speak in the various communities and cities where she had contacts, and also allow plenty of time to tour around and see the countryside. They were excited and happy, but had little time to plan the trip, since they were still occupied with unpacking boxes, entertaining guests, becoming acquainted with local families, earning their trip money, and trying to find someone to dig their storehouse cellar and pour the cement.

In early August the crops began to come in. Will and Linda driving from house to house, sold some of their produce, and local stores bought much of it. Squash of enormous size matured, but were unsalable since most people in the area were not acquainted with squash or did not like it. However, this gave the family a good storable crop for winter use. In a French-English dictionary, Will looked up the names of the vegetables he had for sale and memorized them, so he would be able to identify them as he spoke to people.

About this time, Linda shared a prophecy the Lord had given her regarding the house across the street. They were to own it! A few days later He told Marjorie what the price would be. When they approached the owner, he indicated he had no intention of *ever* selling! The Lord told them to be at peace, and in due time it would all come to pass.

Although the three of them were going in all directions at once, or so it seemed, they met the challenges of each day. One problem—an opportunity, actually (since all problems, they learned, were opportunities)—was that people were asking the name of their ministry. It had no name. The Lord had not given them any. When they asked, He told them to pray and He would reveal it to their hearts.

Thus they were led to choose the name ARC-A-DIA—ARC (promise or covenant), A (in or with), DIA (God). Arcadia— covenant with God! The next day in their overseas mail, the first letter was from Arcadia, South Africa. This seemed quite a "coincidence," since they had just chosen that as their name.

The Lord had also told them to step out each night and view the skies for signs of His second coming, and they had obediently done this. Because of the clear, clean air, the heavens were glorious and could be seen clearly without interference from city lights. Brilliant displays of light were often seen in the apex of the night sky after prayers. Strangely enough, the light could be seen only from the farm. Visitors often drove with the family to the other end of the valley, from which point no sign of light could be seen. A few years later, street lights were installed. Although they were grateful for the lights, they missed the direct view of the heavens.

Since their neighbors on both sides had cows, everyone watched the fences to make sure none of the animals got into the gardens.

Each night, the threesome offered a prayer of protection for their four gardens and the grain fields.

One pitch-black night while Will was still on the veranda viewing the evening skies, he suddenly felt another presence beside him! He said to himself, as his hair rose and his spine tingled, "I feel there is a very *big* presence here with me!" He went quickly into the house, grabbed a flashlight, and returned to find three cows standing motionless beside the porch. One had been practically breathing down Will's neck! At the sudden light, they quickly turned, stampeded through the large garden near the road, floundered through the fence onto the paved highway, and found their way back to their own field.

The next morning, close inspection of the patch where the cows had thrashed through revealed no damage whatsoever. Hoofprints showed that one cow had walked carefully between the rows of tomatoes. God had protected their plants!

Local friends who were familiar with the roads offered to take the family to various sections of the mountain range where occasionally they would find blueberries, as well as high-bush cranberries. On one such trip to the colony site, they discovered currant and gooseberry bushes, loaded and ready for picking.

Garden produce

At pickle- and relish-making time, friends from the village came and everyone went into the fields, then back to the kitchen with their loads of cucumbers, beans, onions, and green peppers. And soon there was the aroma of spices mingled with vinegar as many jars were filled, ready for future enjoyment.

The four large gardens yielded bountifully. More than four hundred squash were picked; onions were pulled and dried and woven into braids to hang in the cellar; carrots and potatoes, parsnips and turnips were dug and stored; corn was harvested; cabbage and the last of the other garden vegetables were picked. Mint grew like ivy and had to be weeded out, but some was saved and dried for tea.

Hay time

From the fields, the harvesters gathered more than two thousand bales of sweet-smelling hay. Most was sold—some was put into their large barn, to help a neighbor who needed storage space.

That first autumn, Linda canned almost sixty jars of applesauce and some cherries, all from the unsprayed orchard next to the grain shed. One day while they were picking apples, they noticed one of the neighbor's cows intently watching them, and they made the mistake of tossing her an apple. As soon as their backs were turned, she leaped over the fence and began to help herself. When Will went to reprove her, she quickly jumped back to her own side. The cows proved to be smart and sassy; they romped and played in the fields like kittens. Needless to say, they presented a comical sight. But this particular one *may* have been the same famous cow that is said to have jumped over the moon!

When October arrived, Will still needed $400 for the trip to England. He had investigated several areas of work, but none seemed right. The jobs required either fluent French or someone for permanent work. At last, one short-term job opened up. The motel in the tourist center in Carleton wanted a house moved. Will had never moved a house—he had no idea how to even begin. But he was the Lord's willing server, and he knew the Lord was with him, so he decided to at least think about it.

With this on his mind, he took his tractor (which had been named Hector) up the mountainside to plow the sloping field. But he was a bit careless and suddenly the tractor turned over and rolled down the hill. Fortunately, Will had jumped free before the machine toppled over.

When he walked back down, Marjorie was working in the barn. She saw his ashen face and knew something terrible had happened. When he told her he might have wrecked the tractor, she first asked, "How are *you?!*"

"Oh, I'm all right," he replied. "I jumped free from the machine before it rolled."

"Then there is nothing to worry about," Marjorie affirmed. "Since your life has been spared, then God will surely fix the tractor." Together they gave thanks for sparing Will's life.

The Lord later pointed out that this had been one of the three temptations each of them must face. YE SHALL NOT TEMPT THE LORD YOUR GOD (Deuteronomy 6:16). Will had taken a chance on the hillside. But no one is to tempt God by doing wrong, thinking to get away with it. Sooner or later it will catch up with that person, and the sooner the lesson is learned, the better life will be. Will had one more major lesson yet to meet, and that was the temptation of power.

A few months later that last temptation was presented. Will was praying when suddenly he was filled with the power of God. He felt so much power he knew he could do almost anything. But he stopped in awe and fear. Such great power would never be safe in human hands. Realizing this, he asked God to remove it from him, and thus Will passed his third test. IT IS WRITTEN, THOU SHALT WORSHIP THE LORD THY GOD, AND *HIM ONLY* SHALT THOU SERVE (Matthew 4:10, italics added).

Since the weather was still fair, with no snow and the ground not yet frozen, the hole for the root cellar was dug and the cement poured by a crew of local men.

The departure date for Great Britain, November 7, was drawing closer each day. On November 2, Will decided to take the job of moving the house, but he insisted that the rest of the family leave without him, since Marjorie had speaking engagements she couldn't cancel. He was packed and ready to leave and would join them over there as soon as his job was finished. The house sitter arrived. Everything was in order—or so they thought!

Marjorie, Linda, Ben, and Betsy (who had just had four baby teeth pulled) were driven to the train, which was due to arrive at 7:00 P.M. Fortunately, they decided to get there half an hour early, for when they arrived at the station at 6:30, the train was about to pull out! When Linda had called, the station master had neglected to say that the train was on daylight time! But it happened to be half an hour late! And so the Lord got His faithful servers and children safely on board, bound for Montreal. On Friday, November 9, they arrived in London, picked up their rented car, and started on their route to fulfill Marjorie's speaking dates.

Meanwhile, Will was still trying to figure out how to move a house. Fortunately it was a small house and several men who had moved houses before offered to assist him. But they all spoke only French! Will prayed "like 60," he said, and by communing with the Lord, learned that he would gain by this experience. He would find that working with the Lord, he was not to depend upon any other power—that of money, prestige, or human beings. All the other help in the world would not move the house. NOT BY MIGHT, NOR BY POWER, BUT BY MY SPIRIT, SAITH THE LORD

(Zechariah 4:6b). This definitely was another growing lesson through which Will came closer to his Lord.

To quote Will: "I found two strong, willing young men to help with the moving, but unfortunately they didn't speak English, and my French was very limited. We spent three days separating the twenty-by-forty-foot part of the building to be moved from the rest of the motel and jacking it up. After receiving advice about how to proceed, we drilled two holes through the floor and underpinning, and attached two large bolts to the structure. The building was placed on skids made of planks nailed together, and a heavy cable was attached to the bolts. The idea was to hook the bulldozer to the cable and drag the building to its new location, one thousand feet away.

"The job sounded simple, because the Lord had provided everything. Laborers were available, experienced advice was available, there was a highway contractor who agreed to pull the building with his bulldozer. Everything was perfect, except . . .

"In speaking with the men, instead of asking for the *shovel*, I asked for the *stove*. The two words are similar in French. My advisors came for only one day, and I couldn't do the job in one day. I felt ill at ease, knowing I had not properly obeyed the Lord by finding work earlier and preparing for my trip, and I was concerned lest I fail.

"But finally the building was ready to move, and I hoped—because of all *my* hard work—the job would soon be finished. The bulldozer hooked on to the cables, moved the building twelve inches, and ripped the skids out from under it. Total disaster!

"I drove my helpers to the restaurant and—not being able to eat—went back inside the building, got down on my knees, and prayed. The Lord had said *He* would move it; I was at the end of my rope, totally defeated.

"However, the Lord gave me the strength to prepare the house again, which we did. We repaired and reinstalled the skids and I asked the road contractor for the bulldozer again. He was busy! Finally a big rubber-tired loader came to do the job. I was heartsick. I said, 'Lord, the bulldozer was a big one, and it had trouble pulling the building. How can this less powerful machine possibly move it?!' Then I remembered: NOT BY MIGHT, NOR BY POWER, BUT BY MY SPIRIT! (Zechariah 4:6). I was then able to release it all to God and, though the machine had trouble, the operator was very skillful and succeeded in finishing the move!

"I received my paycheck for the job, and five minutes before the bank closed, I cashed the check, paid my bills, and had just enough money left to cover my trip. There was no doubt in my mind that all glory and honor belonged to the Lord. What was simple for Him, I had made difficult for myself. My lesson was the same as Marjorie's. *She* couldn't find the farm, and *I* couldn't move the building—but we both knew Someone who could! For these and many other reasons, we can say 'Praise the Lord' and *mean* it!"

Things were not all roses for Will after the house was moved. The plane from Charlo to Montreal was full, so he had to take the train. The heaters on the train had frozen, and when he awoke after a cold, fitful night's sleep, he found himself on a siding in Quebec City, over two hundred miles from Montreal. When he finally arrived and made his way to the airport, he discovered the London flight was overbooked. His only hope was to fly to Scotland and take standby seating on a London shuttle. If he missed his family at Bournemouth, England, they would be on the road and, although he had their itinerary, he wasn't sure how he would find them.

But the Lord is good. Will made it to Scotland, was not bumped off the shuttle, found his way through the maze at London's Heathrow Airport to a train for Bournemouth, arrived there, and took a taxi to the church where Marjorie was speaking.

"Boy, I certainly will try to watch my divine timing from here on!" Will exclaimed as he hugged his wife. He had walked into the meeting just as Marjorie was beginning her talk! It was a time of great happiness as the family was reunited.

CHAPTER TWENTY-ONE

Year One

From Bournemouth they drove to Plymouth, to Biddeford, and on to Penzance. They were particularly interested in the supposed site of King Arthur's castle at Tintagel, on a lonely rocky arm that jutted out into the roaring sea.

Leaving Tintagel, they traveled to Bourne End, Brighton, and London, where Marjorie spoke, then on to visit Stratford-on-Avon, Oxford, and into Wales to Nedbigh Castle. Marjorie's last engagements were at Huddersfield and Manchester in England, where people were responsive and enthusiastic. They seemed to love the Arcadia family and invited them all to come again. Having completed her speaking assignments, Marjorie was free to travel with the family wherever the Lord wanted to lead them.

They drove to Sterling and explored the castle there. It was there that Ben, romping around, might have fallen into a deep stone well if Betsy had not grabbed him in the nick of time. With that, the castle thrill wore off, and they were satisfied to stick to the beaten path. They drove north to Inverness, Scotland, where they visited the famous Pringle Woolen Mills and the beautiful Scottish highlands.

On one of the lovely hillsides, they noticed a flock of sheep with golden fleece! With one accord they all leaned out the windows and stared. The farmer responded to Will's knock on the door. When asked what particular breed of sheep these were, the farmer laughed and laughed. As soon as he had regained his composure, he explained that he had dyed the sheeps' wool to keep track of the rams during mating season!

At Loch Ness, the children called to the Loch Ness monster, but he did not deign to surface.

"Perhaps he is not home today," Betsy joked.

"Or perhaps he isn't there at all!" Linda added.

From the highlands they drove to Glasgow, where they left the car and flew to Dublin, Ireland. There they rented another car and enjoyed the countryside. Will was particularly interested in the crops of sugar beets, rape (a plant of the mustard family), mangel (a variety of large beet), kale.

From Dublin, the family flew back to Montreal. The dear friends in Great Britain would be missed, but they would correspond and see them again. It was good to get back home. The train trip from Montreal to Nouvelle was comfortable, and their house sitter was at the train station to greet them. All in all, it had been a very successful trip!

By Christmas Day the temperature had dropped to 15°, and Will, Linda, Marjorie, Betsy, and Ben huddled by the oil stove in the big kitchen-living room, allowing the oil furnace in the basement to heat the rest of the house. They talked about their accomplishments to date, their hopes and dreams, and the Lord's plans for their work. They enjoyed their beautiful Christmas tree, laden with gifts from friends and relatives, during an evening of joyous sharing.

Christmas sing in the kitchen

Later, all bundled up because as yet there was no heat in the room, they climbed the steep stairs into their chapel. They prayed, read from the Bible, and gave thanks to God for all His blessings. Getting out a paper and pencil, they wrote down a pledge to God and formally dedicated themselves to serve the Lord forever.

Two days after Christmas, Linda held a recital for her piano students. Fifty of their friends and relatives came to the afternoon recital, and another thirty-five attended in the evening. Linda led off with some old-time favorites and hymns, which everyone sang with gusto; then her young students performed, and their parents were pleased. Marjorie tape-recorded the music and played it back for them. Refreshments followed, and everybody had a wonderful time.

One day shortly after Christmas, Will had taken the children to the store in the truck. Linda was stirring something on the stove, and Marjorie was just walking out of the library, when suddenly— without any warning—it seemed to both of them as though the ceiling, roof, and walls of the house had vanished! The two were sharing an open vision together!

They were viewing their mountainside, except that it seemed much higher. The climate was warm and mild, a perfect summer day. Lush forests covered large sections of the mountain range; little vales, sweetly carpeted with emerald-green grass, lay here and there. The grass was like green velvet—unlike anything either of them had seen before. Dells filled with bluebells and other lovely flowers graced the woodland that led gently to other hills.

On the hillside were people beautifully dressed in simple robes, standing relaxed and still in a worshipful mood. The sun was just going down behind the mountains, and the people were meditating on God. But they were not ordinary people. They were a masterful race—not black or white, but of a creamy tan complexion. They were graceful and tall—at least seven feet tall—and there was an air of poised certainty about them. Obviously, they *all knew* GOD personally. An aura of grace and peace on their countenances made them seem one in Spirit, not only with all their own kind, but with the birds and animals that rested peacefully nearby.

Linda and Marjorie were awe-struck, exclaiming out loud to

each other as they pointed out various people, trees, and flowers. A beautiful woman was seated on a mound, playing her harp, as the people listened and pondered their love of God.

As suddenly as the vision had appeared, it vanished. Linda and Marjorie were left in the kitchen, quite astonished by the experience and filled with the joy of it. When they inquired of the Lord as to its meaning, He told them He had wanted them both to witness the kind of people who first inhabited that original part of the world. After man left the Garden of Eden and multiplied, the people were still very conscious of God's glory, dominion, and presence.

The Lord told them that the race had eventually fallen into self-will through disobedience and had been wiped out by other, more savage races. With that change in the nature of man, the environment also gradually changed, becoming more gross in texture. Eventually, destructive elements racked the ranges and changed the face of the earth itself, even before the first polar reverse.

He also told them that He had brought them back to that *particular* farmland because the original race of people had built up a tremendous vortex of prayer power. He said that prayer was cumulative and that this area was set aside as holy ground especially for the purpose of prayer. This was something they could not have done in Sudbury, Massachusetts. Thus the mystery of *why they had to move* was solved!

The new year turned cold. Outside, it was 10° below zero, and only 43° in their farmhouse cellar. Gales whipped around the buildings, and after a few days, the temperature had risen only to 4° above zero. But this did not stop anyone from going to church or to social gatherings. One day some friends drove into the yard in a one-horse open sleigh, singing old-fashioned songs in French. They wished everyone a Bonne Année (Happy New Year), then dashed off down the road at a handsome clip.

The same sleigh returned a few days later; the drivers invited the family for a ride down the valley road to their relatives' home. Huddled under a buffalo robe, they enjoyed the sleigh ride, and their new friends greeted them cordially. They were welcome to visit by their cozy fireside and sip hot chocolate. It seemed that everyone was related to everyone else in the valley, as if they all were one big, happy family.

The weather continued so frigid that the salt-water bay froze and smelt fishing through the ice began in earnest. Will helped some of the men harvest and sell their catch and got plenty of fish for several months' cat food. Linda added vegetables and bread to give the cats a good, hot, nourishing meal, which they enjoyed to the fullest! If Mama Boss Cat could have talked, she would have said "Thanks!" but instead she purred as she gobbled it down.

March brought the end of smelt season, and although snow was still piled high, the days were bright and sunny. Marjorie and Linda were in the yard, sweeping out Will's truck, when they looked toward the driveway and saw their neighbor from across the road walking toward them between the high snow banks.

"Good morning," he announced cheerily. "Do you still want to buy my house?"

Marjorie looked at Linda and Linda looked at Marjorie in shocked amazement. Why was it, that after the Lord had prophesied a certain thing would come to pass, they were always so surprised, when it actually took place?

Marjorie drew in her breath and let it out. "Yes, indeed we do!"

"Well, I've decided to sell it to you," he declared.

"How much do you want for it?" Marjorie asked. Their neighbor named his price, and it was the *exact price* the Lord had told her it would be, long before.

"We'll buy it," Marjorie said without hesitation. "Come in, and we will sign an agreement and make a deposit." The neighbor left happily with the deposit in his hand, and the threesome raced to the chapel to give God the glory and the thanks.

The neighbor wanted to close the deal in two weeks, but they did not have the available cash. This meant they would have to trust God *completely* to produce the money for the purchase *if* He wanted them to have the property for His future use.

By the beginning of the second week, they had the money! Several unexpected rebates had come in the mail, and a friend had sent them a generous personal gift, writing that the Lord had prompted her to send it right away, and she had obeyed. It was

Rainbow House

without fear or doubt that they signed the papers promptly and began renovations across the street. Another of the Lord's miracles had taken place!

March passed into April, with more beautiful white light in the east and the west. Sometimes on a very dark night, the dome of the heavens would be full of light. On April 19, the anniversary of their arrival, the family went up to the temple site to pray and thank the Lord for His great goodness so beautifully witnessed throughout the winter. The Bible was opened and read aloud; Betsy and Ben listened attentively, as well as Sparkie, who sat obediently beside Will. Everyone prayed, and then as they entered into meditation, they observed a strange scene in the large field below them. Apparently seagulls had come to celebrate with them!

At first a few gulls flew in and landed. They walked around, seemed to take stations, and remained silent. Others soon joined them, flying in from different directions, almost as though by divine appointment. As the birds gathered, they received greetings, took their place in the center of the circle, and settled down in silence. In the space of five minutes, all the birds had arrived. It was a very large assembly—in fact, it filled a large section of the

Threesome in prayer at temple site

field. Key birds seemed to be stationed at the perimeter of the circle, standing guard. A crow flew by and was driven away.

The birds remained perfectly silent and stationary for the half-hour the family meditated. As soon as they said "Amen", there was a rustling down below, and the feathered assembly broke up. One by one the seagulls flew off in the directions from which they had come.

Each year the family has gone to the temple site to celebrate on the 19th of April. Although a few gulls have flown by, and occasionally landed, there never has been a reenactment of that strange assembly. There are so many unexplained "coincidences" between birds, beasts, and humans that one sometimes wonders if we will ever gain a thorough understanding of it all!

GREAT IS THE LORD, AND GREATLY TO BE PRAISED IN THE CITY OF OUR GOD, IN THE MOUNTAIN OF HIS HOLINESS. BEAUTIFUL FOR SITUATION, THE JOY OF THE WHOLE EARTH, IS MOUNT ZION, ON THE SIDES OF THE NORTH, THE CITY OF THE GREAT KING (Ps. 48:1-2).

CHAPTER TWENTY-TWO

Spring, Sweet Spring!

After the winter's gales, weeks of below-zero temperatures, and deep snow, spring was eagerly welcomed. Springtime brought fragrances! There were mornings when the air was so filled with the smell of balsam fir, it was like sticking one's nose into a balsam pillow. The herald of spring was clean and pure!

Next came the fragrance of the Balm of Gilead—a rich sweetness that permeated the air, wafting from the big trees by the brook. Then about two weeks later came Miss Strawberry. The wild strawberry plants that covered the mountain sides were in bloom, and the air smelled like a box full of the most delicious strawberries one could ever want to taste. But actually, we tasted them with our noses!

Each special fragrance lasted a week or two, and they were a real delight to Will, Linda, and Marjorie. Although in 1974, this was a very new experience for them, it never ceased to delight as each spring rounded the corner. And by spring, the seedlings that had sprouted in the boxes on the windowsills were growing nicely.

By this time the library shelves had been built, and the boxes of books had been unpacked and filled the walls. The kitchen had been painted and the new stairs to the cellar had been finished.

About that time, Linda had a vision which she shared with the *Messenger* readers: "During meditation this morning, I saw a wine glass. It appeared alone and empty. Then slowly it began to fill up to the top. More glasses appeared and the one glass shared its contents with the others, yet still maintained its own content. Suddenly a man's right arm swept the glasses off their bases. None were broken, but all the wine was spilled out. Then again I saw the glasses, clean and clear, standing upright and attentive as the Lord Himself stood in their midst."

The interpretation: "The glasses are the nations of the world being filled to the brim with wine, which symbolizes, in this particular vision, ungodly indulgences, fleeting and temporal, which humanity increasingly imbibes. The arm was that of Jesus Christ, who alone stands as Lord God of heaven and earth, and who is emptying and cleaning the cups until they sparkle. The erected glasses mean the pure thoughts of life and true joy of the nations—people thus cleansed and prepared for His new heaven and new earth."

THUS SAITH THE LORD GOD . . . I WILL OVERTURN, OVERTURN, OVERTURN IT: AND IT SHALL BE NO MORE, UNTIL HE COME WHOSE RIGHT IT IS; AND I WILL GIVE IT HIM (Ezekiel 21: 26a,27).

The storehouse

With the advent of spring, thoughts again turned to the root cellar and storehouse. Two expert masons put up the walls; they laid 825 blocks in one day. A carpenter put on the roof, and Will gradually finished the interior in the months that followed. This building provided good winter storage for their vegetables, as well as a laundry and toilets, and room to store their extra things upstairs.

Ben, now four years old, was growing—and so were they all, in one way or another. Guests had continued to come, and by June they were ready to greet their first overseas visitor, Richard. In fact, he had traveled nearly eleven thousand miles to get there!

Richard was a Scot the family had met in their travels overseas. He had red hair and a flowing red beard. His job as a social worker did not provide him with much spending money, so he had decided to hitchhike to Arcadia. He accomplished this by getting a job with a group of musicians. He kept their books and did odd jobs, thus earning his passage across the sea, and also across the States. Hitchhiking from Los Angeles to British Columbia and back to eastern Canada gave this young man an invaluable education, as well as a good week's visit with the folks who had inspired his trip.

Richard, Ben and Sparkie

Thinking about his experience at Arcadia, Richard wrote, "I found the community here seemingly at the stage when the seed is germinating and beginning to burst forth with life, vigor, and promise. Even in these few days there were wonderful changes to be seen and felt, both in and around me and also in my own spirit. . . . I was so glad I could be a little help to Will with his monumental tasks of building and cultivating around the farm. My muscles are aching, but my heart is singing!"

Richard did his stint with the Gravely cultivator, among other jobs, and found it a real challenge, since he was not used to that particular kind of labor. He was a strong giant of a fellow, and his red hair and beard streamed out in the wind as he tried to till a straight furrow, but the tiller threw him occasionally because he had not learned the skill of balancing it properly. How often we are thrown by simple problems, all because we have not learned how to let their weight shift properly to the Lord!

The summer of 1974 was a glorious one, through deep sharing and praying with a constant flow of visitors from various walks of life. Some came for two or three days, others for a week or a month, and a few for a longer time. Some came to give, some to take. Some had the Spirit of the Lord to share; others came with grave problems in need of healing. The Lord parceled out His good generously to one and all, and everything took place in a cradle of prayer and praise to God.

An interesting thing happened when Will planted his wheat very late, around the Fourth of July. He wondered whether he should plant at all, but the Lord continually assured the family that it would be good wheat and useful. As summer advanced and the other grains ripened and were harvested, while the wheat looked beautiful, it still was not ripe.

Long after the other farmers' wheat had been safely gathered into their barns, Will wondered what possible use there could be for his unmatured grain. They inquired of the Lord and were again assured that it had a purpose. But it seemed so doubtful, Will called his neighbors for advice. On October 12, the farmer to their left came and shook his head. It was no good! If cut, it would only mold. The farmer on their right came and shook his head also. If it were not cut and left in the field, the straw would cause a problem when Will tried to plow it in. In other words, *if* they cut it, they would have problems—and if they *didn't* cut it, they would have problems! The farmers went home.

Again the Lord's advice was sought, and still He maintained that the wheat had a good purpose and would bring them profit. As they wondered in their hearts how this could possibly be, the idea came to them to contact a dried-flower company in Ontario. Maybe—just maybe—it *might* buy the grain. The company was called and a sample sent. The company was delighted and put in an order for the entire field.

Marjorie gathers the harvest

By that time the wheat had ripened a bit more, and on November 3 it was cut, dried flat in the barn, and prepared for shipment. Will, Marjorie, and Linda cut off the excess stalks and packed the sheaves in florist's boxes. The project was not finished until January 1, because Will had been teaching school full time. There was snow on the ground and the barn was cold, but it was with a feeling of joy that the three took the 139 boxes to the railroad station and saw them off to Ontario.

The next year they raised an earlier wheat crop for the same purpose. That year the company sent them a gift basket containing dried flowers from five countries—Canada was represented by Arcadia Farms wheat!

Although Arcadia had sold some of its wheat to the flower company that year, some was also put into its bins for food. The beautiful golden kernels flowed like sand from the elevator that gathered it out of the truck and hoisted it to the second floor of the barn for storage. And thus began the delicious home-baked bread made with their *own* wheat flour.

Will putting wheat into bins

It was possible to have flour not only from wheat, but also from rye, barley, and buckwheat, since Will had assembled the grain mill Marjorie had brought. This meant all kinds of goodies were available—buckwheat pancakes with golden maple syrup, rye or barley bread, wheat cookies, rolls, cakes, or what have you. It was certainly a treat to be around when Linda took four golden loaves from the oven!

Ben welcomes Mama's bread

Guests not only enjoyed Linda's bread, but her jellies and jams as well. One morning when their sleepy visitors had gathered around the table for breakfast, Linda left the room to answer the telephone. Someone asked for the jam, which was missing from the table, so Marjorie took an already-opened jar out of the refrigerator.

When she and the guest looked at the contents of the jar, he questioned whether it was jam, but Marjorie felt sure it must be, although it was unusually dark. The guest spread a generous amount on his toast and bit into it, only to find that it was a dab of leftover chocolate pudding which Linda had put away in a jelly jar! That became a standard joke with visitors.

Every summer there were struggles with potato bugs which seemed to appear from nowhere overnight. One day the plants would be thriving, and the next, hordes of bugs would be devouring them. Since Arcadia had been called to farm organically, balancing the soil naturally, poisonous sprays were not used. This meant that everyone took turns picking bugs and egg clusters from the plants. Even an occasional visitor offered to take part in this messy exercise, but one needed a particular tenacity, a strong stomach, and a real desire to serve on the Lord's property!

Arcadia had a children's camp that summer. Friends came and brought their children to a week of intensive Bible study from a child's point of view. The children sang and danced to songs which Linda composed; Will took them for tractor rides and trips into the mountains; and Marjorie took them to the beach and helped them write their own little skits.

One skit was about Daniel and the lions' den. Four-year-old Benjamin took the part of King Nebuchadnezzar, an older boy, Don, read from the Bible back stage, and another, Pat, took the part of Daniel. Everyone thought the big barn would make the ideal theater, so bales of hay were moved onto the main floor for seats, leaving a level space for a stage. Mounds of hay on either side of the stage provided secluded "offstage" space.

The excitement of finding costumes led the mothers to large boxes of outgrown clothing. Betsy considered being a queen in a fancy gown, but discarded the idea when she realized it didn't fit the script. Ben dressed up in a blanket tied at the waist with a bright ribbon and wore a crown of gold-colored cardboard.

After much rehearsing, the big day arrived. Parents and children gathered at the barn after dusk. The big lights were turned on and excitement filled the air. The program began with prayer, Linda led the group in songs of praise, a few Proverbs were pantomimed, poems were read by various people, and then—the play!

The main actor, Daniel, lay on the stage. The overhead lights were turned off and a flashlight from the audience assumed the role of a floodlight. The dim flicker of another flashlight could be seen behind the hay bales as Don, offstage, read the story from the Bible. . . . It was time for the king to enter (lions roar!).

A thin voice (Ben's) spoke offstage: "Daniel, are you all right?"

Pat: "Oh yes, O king. The lions didn't eat me! I had faith in God!"

Thin voice: "Are you *sure* you are all right, Daniel?"

Pat: "Yes, O king."

Thin voice: "I must see for myself!"

At that point the bulb in the flashlight burned out. Everyone strained trying to see what was going on. A small dim figure, Ben's, could be seen entering the stage from the left. Then he stepped in a hole and the crown slid down over his face as he disappeared between the hay bales.

It was a tense moment, and the audience held its breath as there was a muffled thrashing about. Finally the thin voice was heard faintly, "Does anyone have a light?"

CHAPTER TWENTY-THREE

Farming in Earnest

There was much laughter as well as many tears that summer and the summers that followed. One child received her first spanking when she spitefully threw a toddler's pacifier into the bull pasture next door. Many requested counsel and prayer help. There were singles, married couples, people with health problems, and others who just came to see what Arcadia was all about and offer help.

On one occasion the two children had been assigned to help a visitor bring his things from his car. As they passed through the family room and up the stairs, Betsy, age nine, carried his shaving kit and Ben, age four, carried his hat. The friend smilingly reported that before he had taken his suitcase from the car trunk, Betsy had questioned, "You certainly must have more than this. Where are your pajamas? If you forgot those, you'll have to sleep in your hat!"

Betsy and Ben loved the Bible stories, and one night as Linda closed the book after reading about Adam and Eve, Ben rolled over to go to sleep, muttering, "Everything was good till Eve ate that tree! What a mess she got us into! *Yuck!*" To which Betsy replied, "That's right, Bennie, *now* what do we do?"

Everyone enjoyed going to the barn to see the cats and kittens and watch the antics of the two new goats. Mandy was Arcadia's first goat. Will and Linda had driven out on the Gaspé one night to fetch her. When they arrived, her owner had trouble finding her. Where was Mandy?—high up in the apple tree, eating apples.

Mandy proved to be a fine goat, with a glossy brown and white coat and a regal air. The other female, Tinkerbell, was purchased later from a farmer in their own valley. She was as flighty as Mandy

Goats and sheep

was stable and never ceased to amuse the family and their guests. Both goats were bred, and each had two kids. Tinkerbell became overly fond of her daughter, Daisy, and spoiled her much as a doting mother would spoil a child.

One day the goats and their kids, now fully grown, were in the pasture and the family was sitting casually on the lawn with some visitors, having a Bible lesson. Around the corner came Tinker-bell, bleating and motioning with her eyes and body for them to follow. Will and Marjorie ran after her as she tore down to the barn, around the corner, and out toward the pasture.

There she ran directly to the fence, sobbing and butting, trying to free Daisy, who had foolishly stuck her head through the wire and was caught by her horns. As soon as Will freed Daisy, Tinkerbell took her to one side and comforted her, tenderly licking and nuzzling.

Mother love was exhibited by Mandy in an entirely different way. Her babies, when small, were trained to do exactly the right thing at the right time, or they received a swift butt from mama! No ifs, ands, or "butts" about it—the goats were interesting animals!

That was the beginning of the Arcadia herd, to which sheep were later added.

Then came chickens. But they had no coops, and their chickens were to be delivered in the spring of 1975. A nearby farmer was disposing of two coops his flock had outgrown and offered them free of charge, but the family wondered how they would transport them—they certainly were too large to fit into the truck.

One summer day Marjorie was on her way down the road with Betsy and Ben for a cool dip in the river. As they neared the bridge, they were amazed to see the farmer's son driving his tractor up the road toward them, pulling a trailer with a chicken coop on it. Behind him was another tractor and trailer with another coop, and behind that came the farmer and the other members of his family in a truck.

The love and friendship of the French people in the area was not only touching, but a real lesson for Americans who had grown up in a "sophisticated" society. Here were simple, honest, God-fearing folk who loved their neighbors as themselves—another revelation from God to man!

As autumn neared, the Arcadians realized they would need a winter coop for the chickens, which were now close to becoming laying hens. Short of funds, they asked the Lord for a little help, and a week or so later they were led to go the beach. A storm at sea had washed a large amount of lumber onto the shore, free for the taking, so they loaded enough into the truck for a good coop! The Lord was teaching them to *"Look to see what you have in supply."*

Betsy and Ben feed the chickens

The Lord's hand had been leading Will into different jobs, teaching him about the country and its good people. He had worked as a truck driver and as a house mover, and then was led to a job as an automobile mechanic. He had a natural ability with cars, but was not a skilled mechanic. Applying at a tire outlet with a service garage attached, he landed a job changing tires and installing mufflers. There was only one thing unusual about that job—the next day the other two employees quit, and Will was the only "mechanic"! Suddenly every kind of repair job was thrust upon him!

One day he found himself on his back under a car, attempting to replace a certain part. Try as he would, he just could not get the broken part out. Finally in desperation, he asked God to help him, and when he again reached up, the part yielded easily and the new one went into place.

Will worked at the garage for several months. Then, having learned what the Lord was teaching him through that job, he was led to a different one—teaching school! In the eight years that followed, Will taught auto mechanics, data processing, Quebec law, English, history, biology, general science, morals and religion, math, social studies, and introduction to technology. He found the children receptive to a father image as he tried to provide counsel and help where it was needed. This was a way of ministering he had not foreseen!

The following spring the family became aware of the startling fact that the middle of their house was collapsing! Because the supporting timbers had been removed to make one big room, the second floor was sinking fast. Something had to be done. In their need, they again sent out a prayer to the Lord. Then Will got a bright idea.

"God sent the lumber for the chicken coop onto the beach for us," he said. "Why can't He wash a beam or two down the brook for the house?"

"Of course He can!" Linda and Marjorie agreed, and they thanked Him in advance.

The Brook

It was flood time, and the next day, when Will walked to the brook, there resting on the shore were two beautiful, hand-hewn beams, just the right strength and length—twenty feet!

"Thank You, Lord," Will said out loud. There was no question in anyone's mind Who had produced the lumber for the repair. But after all, it *was* the Lord's house!

Will hired a carpenter to help him jack up the house and put one huge, heavy beam in place in the center of the family kitchen-living room. It was later removed and used in the next room, and two larger beams were bought to replace it. After a great deal of pushing and shoving and jacking and lifting, they managed to get one end of a twenty-foot-long timber in place, but they needed another pair of hands and more brawn. Then in walked David, Marjorie and Linda's friend from Maine, and his wife, Lynn.

Marjorie greeted them with a brief, "Hello—did you bring your work clothes, David?" To which David replied that he had. He raced to the bathroom, threw on some coveralls, and ran out to grab the other end of the beam and guide it into place. That was the beginning of a wonderful friendship between Will and David that has lasted over the years. As Will explained, he couldn't really lay things down to shake hands, but he certainly was happy to see a new face, especially at that moment!

That same room was the center of much activity. The former owners often came by to visit, together with their friends. When they arrived for one of those visits, Linda was frying something on the stove. They all began to talk and Marjorie and Linda took the visitors out to show them the garden. As Will was pointing out the raspberries, the former owner walked by the front of the house. As he passed the open front door, he looked in and said, "I believe you have a fire!" Will, Marjorie and Linda rushed in to see flames shooting toward the ceiling from the fat in the pan—Linda had forgotten to turn off the burner! Will quickly used the extinguisher and Marjorie threw on baking soda. The flames were put out, leaving scars that had to be sanded and repainted. But the Lord had preserved His building!

Fire was one thing of which the people of that land were extremely wary. Long fire trails wound into the forests, and everyone kept a careful watch, lest a fire get started that might be impossible to stop. One night as Linda, Marjorie, Betsy, and a guest were looking out the library windows, they saw a blaze start in a neighbor's woodland and spread rapidly to the top of the mountain.

Linda suggested that the four of them pray that the fire cease. This they did, putting their faith in God's will. As they watched, the fire died down and went out. They were learning that there is no area in which prayer does not work. Not only were they to pray that the world's people have faith in God's power, but they were to exercise that faith themselves.

There were many things the family needed to accomplish to make the property useful for prayer-community purposes. Will was guided to drill a well in the storehouse cellar, but after some months and several sinkings of his wellpoint, could strike only a ledge. He requested that Marjorie pray with him for further guidance. The Lord told them *exactly where* to put down the pipe, and sure enough, it sank into water that was plenteous and pure.

There were other opportunities to demonstrate the power of prayer. The house across the street had been redecorated, each room in a different color, so it was named Rainbow House. It became empty as summer visitors dwindled and fall visitors moved into the main house. But it soon became evident that Rainbow had a roomer!

A porcupine had moved into the cellar through an open window and had made a nest under a forgotten chair. How does one get rid of a porcupine? Especially one who has decided to move in for a long winter nap? That was the question of the day.

Turning to Marjorie, Will asked, "What shall we do?"

"That's simple," she replied. "Pray!"

And pray they did. They asked the Lord to tell them what to do and to help them do it. He responded by telling them to go over to the house and call down the cellar stairs, telling the creature, in Jesus' name, to leave immediately!

Will in the lead, with Marjorie and Linda trailing, proceeded across the road into the house and peered down into the cellar with a flashlight. Yes, the creature was still there, cuddled comfortably under the chair, with a thousand quills, it seemed, sticking out on all sides.

They spoke firmly to it in the name of Jesus, telling it that it must leave and return to its rightful home in the woods. They closed the cellar door quietly and thanked the good Lord for taking care of the matter. No one wanted to harm the creature. This was the best way possible. Returning the next morning, they found the cellar empty; the stranger had departed for its native haunts!

The little corner store was very handy. Linda would ride down on her bike, with Ben holding on tightly behind her and Betsy trailing on her little red bike. On one occasion, they heard a tiny kitten mewing in the bushes beside the road. They were told by the storekeeper that it was a stray and that Ben could have it. Ben was delighted and gathered the orange and white kitten close in his arms. From then on Cuddles was Ben's cat, and a close relationship sprang up between them. She followed him around much like a dog—went on walks with him, played in the sand pile, and slept on his bed. Cuddles is still a fine cat and considered part of the Arcadia family.

That fall Linda glanced out the front window one day to see Will's mother, Agnes, and a friend, driving into the yard. She called to Marjorie in the kitchen and glanced quickly at Ben, sitting on the couch. Naturally, she wanted him to present a good appearance for his favorite "nanny." She was aghast at what she saw.

"Mom—come quick! Look at Ben!" Ben was covered from head to foot with little red spots.

Linda and Marjorie knew that Jesus taught that good health was the natural state of man, and He proved this by healing all kinds of disorders. Quickly they prayed for Ben's healing, calling upon His "overcoming power." By the time they welcomed their visitors and brought them into the house, the red spots had disappeared and Ben appeared healthy—and he continued to be healthy. Good health was expected at Arcadia!

Marjorie took Agnes upstairs to her room, and the two mothers sat down on the bed together. Much had transpired since they had last seen each other; a sweet love filled them both.

Agnes sighed, "I feel a great peace here. You feel it here, too, don't you." It was more a remark of discovery than a question.

"Yes," Marjorie replied, and the two mothers embraced. Although the Sudbury parting of family ties had been difficult for everyone, prayer had been victorious and family oneness had continued to develop on a deeper and more holy level as the years unfolded. Ralph and Agnes (Will's folks) respected their son for heeding his Lord's call, and they gladly responded in every way. Agnes and her friend spent a pleasant few days in the peace of God's presence, visiting with the family and learning more about the Arcadia ministry.

CHAPTER TWENTY-FOUR

Lost in a Wilderness

Linda loved to celebrate birthdays, so everyone who happened to have a birthday during a visit was the recipient of cards, cake, and all the fixings. One woman in her fifties, from the Midwest of the United States, was especially moved. She had never had a birthday celebrated like this before and was deeply touched. Her eyes became moist with appreciation as the family sang "Happy Birthday."

On special occasions, they also had homemade ice cream. After much churning and freezing, everyone declared it was the smoothest, sweetest, most delicious ice cream ever tasted. Betsy and Ben not only helped with the churning, but enjoyed the fruits of their labors.

By 1975 Ben was making up his own column for the *Messenger*. He told his mother to write down "Humble thoughts make good stories." He might have been small then, but he has since become a handsome, humble, and gifted teen.

That was the summer the threesome decided to open a retreat on beautiful Cape Cod. It was so successful they continued the practice for the next two years. The good Lord always provided the right house-sitters and the family was happy to return to their home state to serve.

One day that same summer, as the family crossed the bay on the ferryboat, they discovered what the Lord meant when He had prophesied that their home would be *"beyond the water banks."* There they were! High above towered banks loaded with rare fossils.

Arcadia retreatants at Cape Cod, Mass.

That year the old metal garage, where the tractor had been stored, was singled out for renovation. Two nice guest rooms with bath and a roomy office for Marjorie were planned. Summer visitors aided in pouring a new cement foundation. Then came the problem of the building. Who would build the office and guest house, later to be named Peace Haven?

Will hired a carpenter to help him. The first day, the carpenter showed Will how to frame the office. The next time, he gave further instruction, and then told Will he couldn't stay. He had another job and then was going to retire. Will was left standing there, wondering how to proceed, as he watched the carpenter drive off. Of course, if one never has a challenge, one never grows—as the Lord had often pointed out! So with Marjorie helping and directing the construction, Will carried on.

Visitors help cement the office floor

When it was time to put the roof on, they heard of a man who had some used tin roofing for sale. Will and Marjorie went to the man's house, bought enough to cover the entire roof, went home, and put it on. Not all their lessons came easily. They discovered that when it rains, "used" tin makes a good shower head.

Each year Marjorie would speak in various parts of the United States—Chicago, Iowa, Arizona, California, Maine, Massachusetts, and Connecticut—as well as in Montreal and western Canada. During these trips she spoke to many kinds of groups, in homes, churches, and public meeting places. Occasionally Will and Linda accompanied and assisted her.

As the months went by and mail was received, they found the quantity rapidly mounting. The Lord gave them a prayer for blessing the incoming mail and the outgoing answers. It was always a thrill to open the mail and see who was writing to them and what problems were in need of prayer.

One day they received a package from England containing a magnificent hand-woven tapestry. A note accompanied it, saying that the sender had heard of them and had woven the tapestry for

Will and Linda in California

their chapel. In the center of the blue background was a beautiful cross of gold, with gold and rose rays—almost like living heart-throbs—radiating from it. This masterpiece has been enjoyed over the years.

From time to time there were mail strikes, and then the three-some had to find ways to send their outgoing mail on its way. It required much diligence to attend to all the varied details of founding their ministry. The Lord was teaching them that *"for every difficulty there is a victory!"*

The Lord explained to them, one day during devotions, *"My hurting body is humanity, but if every Christian would be a walking Christ, my body soon would mend. Thus ye each has work to do!"*

As the many team members moved out into the field, the word was spread and the threesome found the Lord had strange and wonderful ways of returning the blessings they were giving out in His name.

Their Arcadia "family" was growing throughout the United

States and Canada, into Europe and Africa, and beginning to reach around the world by word of mouth and friendship. Since they had a surplus of jellies and jams made from the fruit of their prolific apple orchard, strawberry beds, and raspberry plants, plus their own organic flour, the Arcadians developed the custom of sending "goodie" boxes to special friends who had helped them through the year and to shut-ins and lonely people. It was beautiful to see the long kitchen table loaded with jars in pretty Christmas wrap, and later, the attractive boxes prepared for mailing. All this was done freely, for the fun of spreading the joy of the Lord.

Christmas boxes

Although good health was expected, some challenges were not met instantly. One evening Will suddenly felt ill—so ill he couldn't stand up, but stretched out right on the kitchen floor, groaning. Linda and Marjorie knelt beside him, praying for the illness to pass. Suddenly Marjorie, who was facing the window, saw two heads flash by. Visitors were approaching the front door and would soon come in! People there never knocked or locked their doors. They just opened the door and walked in. That was the custom.

When the door opened, Will leaped to his feet and greeted the visitors with a smile, then bolted for the bathroom. It was a jerky greeting, to say the least, and the following conversation was repeatedly interrupted as Linda and Marjorie took turns staying with Will in the other room. In their best French, they tried to explain that he was not well, but were not too successful until he returned, white, and soon left for the last time that evening. The illness was overcome by prayer, and the next morning he felt fine.

Winter—Will plowing out

166

More people began to hear about the Arcadia World Prayer Ministry. Some came during the summer months but others wanted to see *real winter*. One family from California asked if they could arrive in February. They outfitted themselves with ski suits so they could try out their snowshoes and see the country—not first hand, but first foot!

Snowshoeing was a sport all could enjoy. Taking Ben on his back, Will would hike with Marjorie, Linda, and Betsy along the pasture road to the brook and back again. Occasionally Marjorie and Linda would hike up to the temple site, a good mile away. It was fun to walk on top of the snow, over the drifts and in the wide-open spaces, after being cooped up in the warm house!

Winter fun

As spring approached, friends took them to a maple grove in the deep woods not far away. Snow was still on the ground—in fact, the owner of the grove had to shovel out his hut, which lay deep in the drifts. Snowmobiles came and went with buckets of sap from the maples. These were poured into two huge buckets which, in turn, ran into large vats over log fires.

Everyone tasted the sap direct from the tree, again later after it had boiled a bit and was syrup, then when it had become taffy. They dribbled spoonfuls over piles of snow on the tables so it would harden quickly, then ate it. As the syrup became sugar, they marveled as the fragrant steam poured out the window. But of the sugar, they could find no adjective to adequately describe its pure sweetness. If only God can make a tree, only man can make sugar from it!

Mountain Wilderness

Summer guests were asked not to wander off alone in the woods. Arcadia was in a valley, edged on three sides by wilderness. One visitor, Bob, was an avid hiker. He mentioned that he wanted to take a walk after supper, but was told of the deep woods and ravines and was persuaded to take a bike ride on the paved road instead.

As the rest of the crowd still sat around the table talking, they saw him ride past the window. He had said he would return for 8:00 prayers in the chapel. But 8:00 came and went—as did 9:00, 10:00, and 11:00. The group, becoming concerned, began to call local hospitals, and some set out in cars to search. No one had noticed which direction he had taken, and no trace could be found of the bike or of the young man.

By midnight, neighbors previously alerted called to see whether he had returned. Upon hearing that he had not, they organized search parties and soon lights were seen on the mountains. The territory was being combed, because they knew the dangers of wandering aimlessly on those mountains alone in the dark. Others beat their way through the bushes along the river, hoping he had not by some chance accidentally fallen in. Someone suggested they call the border to see if by any chance Bob had decided to hitch-hike back to the States, but no one answering his description had shown up. One o'clock came and passed.

At 2:00 A.M., after much prayer, Marjorie stood in the front door of the farmhouse and spoke calmly and firmly in the Spirit, "Bob, wherever you are, hear my voice, and in the name of Jesus, return here *immediately!*"

At 3:00 A.M. Bob walked in the front door and greeted Marjorie joyfully. He said he had ridden the bike down the road until he came upon an interesting path. Dragging the bike into the under-brush, he had left it and set off on foot. As twilight faded into dusk, he suddenly realized he could not find his way back to the road. He was lost! He did not know how long he wandered and thrashed around in the underbrush, going in circles and falling into panic.

Then after a long time, he clearly heard Marjorie telling him to come home. Following her voice, he knew in which direction to walk. Eventaully, he came back to the place he had entered the forest, got on the bike, and pedaled back. Bob was a disheveled and shaken young man, and the rest learned from his experience. However beautiful it might be in daylight, one does not venture into the wilderness after dark. Survival is not easy for beast or for man. Wild animals, as well as sudden dropoffs into deep chasms with spring-fed waterfalls are numerous. By the grace of God and through much prayer by everyone in the group, Bob's life had been spared.

The natural beauty of the countryside afforded many opportunities to commune closely with God. Prayers and devotions took place wherever the people found themselves at prayer time. Sometimes they were on the beach, at other times, in the fields, the barn, or on the mountainside.

One night the group held evening vespers in the deserted colony area. Getting into their cars, they drove carefully up the steep, winding, narrow mountain roads until they reached the top. The sun was just dipping in the west, but there was still enough light to read the Bible. They meditated upon its words, and then sent out prayers for the world's people.

The sun set, and they sang hymns as it grew darker. One man played a beautiful flutelike tune on a recorder as everyone listened quietly. The evening light was soft, like velvet. A lovely white bird circled above the group, swooping lower and lower toward the man with the recorder until it finally fluttered right above him. Then it flew off. It was a beautiful experience for everyone.

One night later on, after prayers in the chapel, the group walked outside to view the glory of the heavens. Above them a white light in the shape of a giant hand with five clearly defined fingers hovered in the heavenly apex. On another occasion there was a most beautiful display of white and flame-colored lights above the brick house. These were not the northern lights, which were seen occasionally. These lights lasted long enough for those outside to go in and gather others to view the sight. Only when the visitors saw with their own eyes did they believe the report.

CHAPTER TWENTY-FIVE

An Organ for the Chapel

On the morning of March 6, during chapel service, the Lord showed both Marjorie and Linda, in vision, a small organ standing in the corner of the room. After meditating on the Lord's Word there was a time of sharing, and they both told of seeing an organ in the room. Will threw up his hands and roared with laughter. It was the height of absurdity! Never could anyone—*anyone*—ever get an organ into *that* room!

In the first place, he said, the door from the main house was just too narrow. In the second place, the stairs from the shed below were too steep and the opening in the floor too narrow. A human body could hardly get in—much less an *organ*! And in the third place, there was no extra money for organs. He added, and *who* would ever think to *give* them an organ? With that, nothing more was said. The subject was dropped.

It is interesting to observe how human logic can try to discredit the Lord's will and wisdom. Will was right in his reasoning, but their Lord was not limited to material conditions. He was the Lord of Spirit and of Divine Will. If He had decided there would be an organ in His chapel, then His hand would not be shortened! Material conditions would just have to yield to His will!

Three months later the Arcadians received word from friends in the Midwest that they had a small upright electric organ they wanted to give Arcadia for its chapel. What news! The threesome met and praised God. They accepted the gift and then set to work to decide how they would get it into the room. Will offered to drive the truck to Iowa and bring the organ back for the Lord's work!

Linda playing the organ in the chapel

When he arrived with it, they carried it up the stairs, and it cleared the opening by ¼ inch!

The organ still stands as a memorial to the Lord's promise that March morning. Its sweet melodious tones fill the air as Linda plays it beautifully and the guests sing, "For thine, O Lord, is the kingdom and the power and the glory, for ever and ever. Amen!"

When June came in 1976, it seemed to burst forth all over— with 80° and 90° temperatures, lilacs, apple blossoms, sweet breezes, and cloudless skies. And usually there was a nest of new kittens to be found.

One day Ben tried to take his dad to the barn. "Daddy, I want to show you the baby kittens."

Will replied, "Yes, Ben, I've already seen them."

Ben: "But you haven't seen them the way *I'm* going to show them to you!" Who could say no to such a sweet little boy?

At times Betsy did not think he was so sweet. Exasperated

beyond control, she sputtered one day, "Why did Ben have to be born so young!"

Even in his school class he was one of the youngest, since his birthday was in September. But on kindergarten graduation day he felt equal to his peers. Twenty little boys and girls marched down the aisle in caps and gowns to receive their diplomas. When it was Ben's turn to walk forward, he couldn't move. Someone was sitting on his robe! After the ceremony the little ones assailed the refreshment table like a swarm of blackbirds.

Peace Haven visitor house and office

At the end of the busy summer, fall plans included replacing the office roof with new tin, and flooring and insulating the attic. Guests offered to help, and the crew began to work at 7:00 A.M. But the job took much longer than they expected, the temperature began to drop, and the atmosphere was charged with impending snow.

Stopping only to eat, they worked all day and into the night, praying to the Lord to hold off the snow. From time to time, Linda brought the tired crew hot soup, coffee, and cocoa, and at last the job was finished. At 5:00 A.M. it began to snow and formed drifts that did not melt until spring. That was the year the snow came almost to the second-story windows, even as their friends had humorously warned them.

Linda did not work on the roof with the others. She had not been feeling well and discovered she was pregnant with their third child. At the beginning of the pregnancy there were complications, and the doctor suggested that an abortion would be the safest medical procedure.

Immediately, Linda and Will tuned in to the Lord and both received the same answer: *"Do not have an abortion."* They refused to be responsible for taking the life of their child. They asked for an alternative. The doctor said he would do his best to correct the problem surgically, but he could guarantee nothing. The operation was successful, but Linda was required to take it very easy indeed for quite a while.

That was the beginning of prolonged rest and seclusion for Linda, while Marjorie cared for the children, got meals, took Linda's food to the second floor, and harvested the garden, until friends came to help.

One noon, Marjorie asked Linda what she would like to eat. Linda replied, "Raspberry yogurt with peaches on top." On the counter beside the refrigerator was a container that looked like a yogurt carton, and its contents were raspberry colored. Putting some in a bowl and spreading peaches on top, Marjorie had started up stairs when the Lord told her to sample it. Marjorie took a big spoonful and discovered that the container had held Will's hand cleaner! It was awful stuff and she bolted downstairs to spit it out. Fortunately, *she* had taken the first taste!

Through much care and prayer, Linda was able to retain the baby, and on May 16, 1977, beautiful John Andrew Hawes was born. The birth was extremely difficult, but with prayer support from the team members, Linda came through safely. Will remained by her side throughout the whole birthing process, and when they saw the precious baby the Lord had given them, they were glad they had saved his life.

Six months later Linda again did not feel well. She was still nursing and thought she could not have become pregnant—but

John Andrew Hawes at age 2½

she was! On August 25, 1978, Samuel David Hawes came into the world—a bright individual from the very beginning!

During these pregnancies the Lord told them that He is the Creator who gives the gift of *life*. There are times when conditions are such that a mother's life must be saved by abortion, *but that is rare*. He also told them that after He created souls, they need to be born into the world for the purpose of Spiritual evolvement. If fetuses were aborted indiscriminately, these souls are denied entrance. Further,

John and Sam in 1985

175

Betsy and Ben in 1985

he said that abortion in general is an abomination before God. Will and Linda thanked the Lord of life for their four lovely children.

At the date of this writing, John Andrew is seven—a tall, beautiful boy with a bright spiritual mind and an agile body, loving and kind, with an appreciation of the good earth. Samuel David, at six, is small and wiry, inventive and clever, a prankster ready to press his luck to the limit, but with such a big heart he loves one and all. Without these two important people, the family would indeed have been incomplete!

The Lord loves all His children—both large and small. When Betsy was small, she slept in the bedroom across the hall from her parents. One night she woke them, complaining of an odor in her room. They drowsily told her to go back to bed, which she obediently did.

But soon she was back—"There is an awful smell in my bedroom." Will told her to close her window, perhaps it was coming

176

from outside. She told him the window wasn't open. He dragged himself to her room, noticed no peculiar smell, tucked her into bed again, and told her to go to sleep.

A short while later she again woke them, saying the smell was like smoke. Would they please come and investigate? This time boths parents noticed an acrid odor. Linda ran downstairs to check the kitchen and cellar while Will hurried to the child's bedroom. Examining the bedclothes, he found that the electric blanket had been tucked under the mattress, short circuited, and set fire to the mattress. Fortunately there was a plastic sheet over the mattress which contained the flames, and which also gave off the smell that caused the alarm. Will quickly pulled off the bedclothes and carried the mattress downstairs. Linda and Marjorie took it outside while he rushed back to see whether anything else was burning.

During the next few days Marjorie patched the mattress and it was again put into use. No odor of fire remained on it or in the room. This was another instance of the Lord's loving protection, which is everywhere, without discrimination. They were aware of that love and called upon it daily.

God's protection extended into the fields. Once when Will was ready to plow the buckwheat field next to the brook, he decided it should first be burned. The threesome, equipped with shovels, brooms, and pails, set fire to the downwind edge of the field, intending to burn a safety zone around its border. The fire burned slowly for quite a time, but suddenly a breeze came up and turned it toward the woods. Linda and Marjorie battled a wall of roaring flames as Will attempted to back-burn behind them. It seemed to be a losing battle—the blaze leaped the trench Will had dug, as well as the burned strip, and was racing toward the nearby trees. They knew that if the trees caught, the fire would spread quickly to the whole mountain, and to their neighbors' forests as well.

With no hope of checking the fire, the threesome panted a prayer aloud, asking the Lord to use His power. Quickly, the wind changed direction, urging the blaze toward the brook, which was too wide to leap, and thus it died out. The Lord proved, time and time again, that by their own power, they just would not make it!

177

Marjorie and Linda shared a similar experience while Will was away teaching school. They had started a very small fire to burn off the clover patch beside Rainbow House, when suddenly a wind sprang up and drove the flames, raging, toward the house. The two battled the fire until they were almost out of breath, and it was about to leap the fence and catch the shingles of the house.

Crying out to the Lord for help, they received their answer—the breeze changed its course and the fire ceased. When they were cleaning up after their escapade, Marjorie discovered that her hair had been singed, and her arms looked like red checkerboards. With prayer, she healed quickly and had recovered by the next morning. They realized that there is an art to fire fighting and that they did not know it; thus it would be better to leave the fires to Will, who by then had become extremely cautious.

Part of God's acreage before and after harvesting

As the years unfolded, summertimes saw the children growing—Betsy entertaining her friends; Ben running from the chicken coop calling, "Here are the eggs, Mother, two hot and one cold!"—and

Will going off to McGill University for further study. More rainbows landed on their fields, and two more tractors, a plow and bucket-loader, a hay baler, a combine, a wagon, and a binder were added. They bought property up the street, visited with friends, took weaving lessons with local weavers. There were lighted evening skies, rock and shell collections, French lessons at the local school. And of course, there were always the animals—and the neighbor's cows!

One night Marjorie was wakened by a mooing outside her bedroom window. Rousing, she realized a neighbor's cows were again out of their pasture. Turning on her light, she saw it was 2:00 A.M. She reached for a robe and called Will who came sleepily down the stairs to phone their next-door neighbor. Will's French was still not very good, but he got his message across by explaining as best he could. Their neighbor and his son got out of bed and the two of them arrived a few minutes later. As they drove the cows down the road toward his pasture, he called good naturedly over his shoulder, "Not my cows!"

It turned out to be true! The cows had come from the field farther on, but the neighbor they had called kindly put them in his own pasture until morning. That's the way it is in this country.

The chickens were always interesting, especially when it was warm enough for them to be outside in the fenced run. The children often discussed whether Henny Penny, their favorite hen, was especially loved by God. It seems that Henny Penny knew a secret way out of the coop which allowed her sole access to Marjorie's strawberry bed. Often she would be found eating strawberries to her heart's content, but always alone. She never let the other chickens in on her secret way of escape.

The others would gather woefully at the fence and watch Henny Penny indulge herself, to their agony. Charlie, the rooster, would crow at her, to no avail. He and his other feathered beauties were inside and Henny Penny was outside, with inside information she was not about to share!

CHAPTER TWENTY-SIX

God Is So Good!

From time to time Linda composed songs and, having been trained in musical composition, would write them down. Occasionally Marjorie would receive a little tune which Linda also wrote and harmonized. Others involved in the ministry wanted to contribute songs, and almost before they knew it, they had enough singable music to compile their first song book. That book, *Arcadia Sings 1*, was published and sold, with the proceeds going to the ministry. A second book, *Arcadia Sings 2*, followed later. Each was beautifully illustrated by artist friends who lovingly contributed drawings, and another dear friend donated hours of skilled proofreading.

Ever since the Israel trip, the threesome had wondered who the special friend the Lord had spoken of would be. Surely, they had either overlooked him or been exceedingly slow to recognize him. They remembered several outstanding people with whom they had become friendly, and more than a year after the trip, one man began writing to them. It seemed that he was an editor and was also artistically talented. After some time, Mr. H told them that if he could be of service in the Lord's work, he would be more than happy to help.

His timing was perfect! Just then they needed an Arcadia seal, and they wanted to use the little drawing the Lord had given them through Marjorie, showing them how to find their farm. Mr. H was sent a copy of the drawing, and he worked out a design, sending samples from time to time for their approval or suggestion. Finally in February 1976, the seal was completed. When the threesome opened the package, they stood awestruck. Mr. H later admitted that he had had divine help in producing the masterful piece of art work. The seal is now copyrighted and appears on all Arcadia Healing World Prayer Ministry stationery, literature, books, pins, and other materials, and is embossed on all legal papers.

The threesome's visions pertaining to various features of their work were usually shown to them long before they came to pass, for the Lord wanted them prepared and successful in all ways. One morning in 1974, Linda was shown a woman she described as having bright, keen eyes, white glistening hair, and an oval face. The woman was very spiritual, with an intense interest in their prayers. She was quiet, ready for prayer, and a capable worker who would be assisting Marjorie, in particular. Usually they had to wait for a vision to unfold, and it was not until 1977 that this one came to pass.

Elizabeth Edwards, a widow, resided in the Midwest, and her work there had come to a halt. She and Linda had never met, nor

Elizabeth Edwards

had Linda ever seen her picture. However, the first time Linda saw Elizabeth, she recognized her as the woman in her vision. Elizabeth had known Marjorie for several years. When invited by the Lord to join the Arcadia Ministry, she decided to accept. This meant a big change for her, but she went to a Canadian immigration office and applied for residency.

The official who interviewed Elizabeth asked why she wanted to live in Canada. She replied that she planned to live with her friends and help in their work. He inquired whether she had ever been there. Truthfully, she had to reply, "No."

"Then how do you know you will like it?"

She assured him that she would like it just fine!

Elizabeth is a woman of great faith, and when the Holy Spirit called her, she had not questioned—her life had previously been given to the Lord. The extent of her faith was well tested before her notification of approval arrived months later. On moving day, her brother and his wife drove Elizabeth, in her own car, crossing at Detroit and following the Trans-Canada Highway as far as Riviere du Loup. It was 3:00 P.M. when her brother and his wife boarded a bus to go back to their home in Illinois, leaving Elizabeth to drive the rest of the way alone.

Continuing east until she saw a sign that indicated a right turn to Mont Joli, which she knew she had to pass through, she drove deeper into Quebec. Her map said she should be on Route 6, but she could not find any Route 6 signs and was puzzled. Asking the way by pointing at the map and questioning, "Numero six?" was also confounding since she was answered in French and could not understand a word. At last in Mont Joli, a motel came into view. She managed to sign up for a room, but could get no understandable road directions until a salesman came up to the counter. He was staying the night, too—and he spoke English! He explained to her that the route numbers had recently been changed, and now Route 6 was Route 132!

Elizabeth was up early the next morning and set out in the rain to follow 132 south, through the same gorge Marjorie had traveled in October 1972 while searching for the farm. The road was under repair, and since it wound through a deep narrow ravine, the detour was beside the regular road. At times it was on the edge, with the rain washing dirt over the sheer precipice; at times it was on the inside of the road, over heaps of dirt, on a path only wide enough for one car—yet it was two-way traffic! Because of the weather, no doubt, no work was being done and there were no flagmen! Yes, she prayed!!—and nothing came from the other direction. Praise God!

After many more miles, Elizabeth emerged at Matapedia and turned east. The paved road widened, and she continued directly to Nouvelle Ouest, where she stopped at a grocery store to call the farm.

In her best French she inquired, "Telefone?" and the clerk handed her their own phone with a smile! Linda, who answered, was overjoyed and came immediately in the farm truck, with John, then six months old, strapped in the seat beside her. Elizabeth followed the truck to the brick house and they went in to become better acquainted. Will was at work teaching school, and Marjorie was on a speaking tour.

That was 1977, the year Marjorie spoke in Maine, then down through the eastern states to West Palm Beach, Florida, back again to Washington, D.C., where she held a service on Christmas Day, then on to Baltimore, and home again. She had given many talks, held many workshops and worship services, and was happy to be back when she arrived for a late Christmas. Needless to say, seeing Elizabeth there was a real joy! Elizabeth was to be Marjorie's private secretary and a true friend!

Before Elizabeth knew whether the Canadian government would accept her as a legal resident it became evident that she and Marjorie would need a dwelling of their own. Pooling their ideas and abilities, they planned a chalet, which had been started during the summer but was not finished when Elizabeth arrived early in November, so Linda put her in Marjorie's bedroom. When Marjorie returned, she slept in the guest house.

The large office in Peace Haven immediately became a hub of activity. Elizabeth began answering mail and typing manuscripts as Marjorie began to write in earnest. Elizabeth was just what the doctor ordered—the doctor, in their case, being the Lord! The threesome was so grateful for this new loyal and peace-filled worker that they never ceased giving God thanks and glory.

The Chalet

Will, Linda, and Marjorie tried to hurry the completion of the chalet by doing odd jobs after the workmen had left for the day. One night, Marjorie, attempting to close the cellar door, saw that the electrician, who had hooked up a temporary line direct from the pole, had left two lines of wire lying in the doorway. Marjorie picked them up, hugged them to her chest, and carried them out under the trees for the night. As she laid them down, she thought they looked rather untidy, and perhaps she should roll them up. But the Lord told her to leave them alone for the night, so she did.

The next morning Will almost had a fit when he discovered she had carried a live line! If she had happened to touch an end, or touch the two ends together, she would have been instantly electrocuted! Once again, the Lord proved that He was guarding them carefully. They needed only to obey that inner prompting, always present through a clear and clean conscience. The Lord had told them that He speaks to all the souls on earth through each person's conscience. This is why it is so necessary that we remain honest, pure, and true to God—we live in a world so haphazard and dangerous.

Our Bible reports that on Mt. Horeb, Elijah discovered the power of the Lord's voice through his conscience: AND AFTER THE EARTHQUAKE A FIRE; BUT THE LORD WAS NOT IN THE FIRE: AND AFTER THE FIRE A STILL SMALL VOICE! (I Kings 19:12).

After months of waiting, in March the day finally came when Elizabeth and Marjorie could move into their new home across the road. The chalet is behind and to one side of Rainbow House, on a slight mound near a cluster of evergreen trees. Moving day was beautiful and cold, with snow on the ground, and the blue mountains hovered in the background as the happy family celebrated with prayer and praise.

Shortly afterward, Marjorie and Elizabeth held open house. They found that the large upper room easily accommodated more than one hundred neighbors and townspeople who came to celebrate with them. It was a wonderful evening. As the village priest blessed the house to the Lord's use, it was beautiful to have everyone join in prayer together, to know that the password of love was a potent element in the promotion of the Lord's work.

The lower level, the basement of the chalet, became a grain center where wheat, barley, buckwheat, and rye was ground into flour and packaged and shipped out for sale. People were happy to receive flour from grain that had been organically grown.

With the completion of the chalet, and later a metal structure for housing farm machinery, and woodworking and metal shops, Arcadia's basic building program was finished. The way was now clear for the founders to channel their energies in other areas, as the Lord directed.

Over the years they have made field trips into the United States, Great Britain, and Europe. People have come for retreats, lectures, and classes offered by the Arcadia staff. However, throughout all these activities, intercessory prayer for the world has remained the first priority.

Today Arcadia Healing World Prayer Ministry is a legal corporate body in Canada. It receives many letters, phone calls, and personal requests for prayer help, and through the work of the Holy Spirit, healings and miracles have taken place. Arcadia believes that works should not be simply talked about, but demonstrated. Since its founding twelve years ago, a branch work called Arcadia School of Light has been established in the United States. This augments their Canadian prayer and Bible-based teaching with an additional field service, world-wide. EVEN SO FAITH, IF IT HATH NOT WORKS, IS DEAD (James 2:17).

From the beginning, the Lord has emphasized that *He* is the head of their ministry, and that the three of them are to act not on their own as individuals, but as a unit. Therefore they must always be in wholehearted agreement as they look to Him for direction and obey it. This they have done, and will continue to do as the years unfold.

ALL THAT THE LORD HATH SAID WE WILL DO, AND BE OBEDIENT (Exodus 24:7b).

CONCLUSION

The past twelve years have seen the beginning of an exciting, rewarding ministry which continues to unfold. As the Lord strides ahead of us, giving detailed instructions, we hasten to follow, trying to let His character infill each of us. We have not arrived at the state of perfection, but we hold to the goal of the teaching of Jesus: BE YE THEREFORE PERFECT, EVEN AS YOUR FATHER WHICH IS IN HEAVEN IS PERFECT (Matthew 5:48).

Eagerly, we anticipate the rise of the glistening white stone Prayer Temple, staffed with its dedicated round-the-clock workers. This and other precious prophecies still await fulfillment.

We happily look forward to the coming of the Lord, Jesus Christ, as He gathers His own to Himself from the far corners of the earth. At the culmination, there will be no earthly labels on God's people. They will be white, black, yellow, tan, red, brown, and will speak the various languages of the earth. They will hail from many places, because God is beyond human descriptions and confinements. God judges by the heart's sincere commitment to Jesus Christ as Lord and Savior, and not by circumstance!

God is love, and we shall fully love as we unite completely with Him. Our whole joy rests in obeying God and in helping others prepare themselves to enter the Lord's new Kingdom—that HOLY CITY . . . COMING DOWN FROM GOD OUT OF HEAVEN . . . . AND THE CITY HAD NO NEED OF THE SUN, NEITHER OF THE MOON, TO SHINE IN IT: FOR THE GLORY OF GOD DID LIGHTEN IT, AND THE LAMB IS THE LIGHT THEREOF (Revelation 21:2b, 23).

THE ARCADIA STORY
QUESTIONS AND ANSWERS

1. WHAT IS THE MEANING OF THE NAME ARCADIA?

ARC-A-DIA means "covenant with God."

2. WHAT IS THE PURPOSE OF ARCADIA?

Arcadia is an intercessory prayer ministry under the direction of Jesus Christ. Its prayers serve to bring healing to individuals and to humanity as a whole, in preparation for the transition into the new Kingdom of God. Tel. (418) 794-2843

3. WHAT DENOMINATION IS ARCADIA?

Arcadia is nondenominationally Christian in its Biblical teaching, believing that there is only one true God for all people and that His only begotten Son, Jesus Christ, is the only door to salvation.

4. CAN VISITORS COME TO ARCADIA?

Visitors may come by invitation or by appointment. Further information may be obtained by writing directly to ARCADIA, P.O. Box 8, Nouvelle West, Quebec, Canada, GOC 2GO.

5. HOW MAY I RECEIVE NEWS ABOUT ARCADIA?

ARCADIA publishes a monthly newsletter, the *Messenger*, available on a love-offering basis.

The Threesome in 1985
Marjorie, Will, Linda

Four children

Betsy, Benjamin, John Andrew, Samuel David, Hawes